Business Studies

Author
John Brand

Series editor
Alan Brewerton

Revision Notes

A level

Letts
EDUCATIONAL

Every effort has been made to trace copyright holders and to obtain their permission for the use of copyright material. The authors and publishers will gladly receive information enabling them to rectify any error or omission in subsequent editions.

First published 1998

Letts Educational, Schools and Colleges Division, 9–15 Aldine Street, London W12 8AW
Tel. 0181 740 2270
Fax 0181 740 2280

Text © John Brand 1998

Editorial, design and production by Hart McLeod, Cambridge

British Library Cataloguing-in-Publication Data

A CIP record for this book is available from the British Library

ISBN 1 84085 100 7

Printed and bound in Great Britain

Letts Educational is the trading name of BPP (Letts Educational) Ltd

Contents

Introduction

- Most students find studying an A level course different from what they have been used to, probably because of the way it is done, usually in small groups, and also because there are the opportunities to tackle topics in more detail.

- The overall aim of a course is to help the student understand the nature and working of business, and to develop key skills – the ability to recognise, define, analyse and evaluate problems. At A level, marks for higher grades need to be gained via **analysis and evaluation**.

- **Case studies**, real and realistic, are used throughout A level courses (whether modular or linear) and they feature in most examinations as well. Many would say that the case studies are what makes the subject so absorbing.

- It is very useful to have done the GCSE course before tackling the A level course, but many candidates starting from scratch enjoy the novelty of the new subject, and are encouraged that the subject seems to be approachable. Practice, followed by real examination questions are then, hopefully, not found to be difficult to understand, although a teacher may quickly point out the large amount of **detail** expected at A level, compared to GCSE.

- Even if you have studied successfully for the GCSE qualification, you may appreciate reminders of basic but fundamental business concepts, and even a summary/reminder of the overall subject content…

Business Studies can be divided into three sections:

(i) The business itself – What type and size? How is it organised? Who are its 'stakeholders'? How are its different departments performing, e.g. Human Resources, Marketing, Production, Accounts? How is it changing? Who is affected, and how?

(ii) The business in the market – How is it reacting to its changing market conditions? Is there enough demand – short-term and long-term? How fierce is the competition? Are there opportunities, e.g. in the Single Market?

(iii) The business in the economy – How is it affected by current trends in the economy, e.g. 'recession' or 'recovery', and resultant government policies, e.g. on tax changes? What are the constraints, e.g. legislation, or competition policy? How will changes in interest rates and/or exchange rates affect it? Are there other political, social and/or legal factors?

Types of businesses

Type 3 is less common, so less likely to appear in the exam papers.

The simplest method of analysing the businesses operating in the UK economy is to divide them into five categories (four of them in the private sector):

1 Sole trader (or sole proprietor)

2 Partnership

3 Co-operatives   (a) retail   (b) producer/worker

4 Limited companies   (a) private   (b) public

5 Public corporations (in the Public Sector).

Think of examples of each type.

Summary of main aspects of types 1, 2, 4 and 5

	1 Sole trader	2 Partnership	4 Limited companies (a) Private	(b) Public [plc]	5 Public corporation
Ownership	By the individual.	By the partners.	By the shareholders – shares *not* available to the general public.	By the shareholders – shares are available to the public (individuals and institutions).	By the State (strictly speaking *not* by the government).
Objectives	Profit, income, job satisfaction, survival (in a recession), 'plough back' for expansion.	[see Topic 2 Objectives]			Provide a public service and (if possible) break-even.
Control	Directly by the owner.	Directly by (at least some of) the partners.	Shareholders elect directors (for three years at a time) ... 'The divorce of ownership from control', but shareholders can vote, e.g. at AGMs, and get Report + Accounts annually.		Government minister is responsible, and reports annually to Parliament. He/she appoints directors.
Use of profits	Income to the owner and/or ploughed back/ reinvested.	Distributed among the partners and/ or ploughed back/ reinvested.	Dividends distributed to shareholders, and/or 'ploughed back'/reinvested, and/or put in 'reserves' (e.g. for a future takeover).		Any 'surplus' is ploughed back, or claimed by the Treasury for the government.
Additional points	Earliest and most common type. Flexible! Less complex, e.g. on tax. But ... **'unlimited liability'**.	Risks spread more, and more capital and skills available? 'Sleeping' and 'limited' partners allowed, but ... overall **'unlimited liability'**.	Often originally, or still, based on a family. Can be very large. 'Ltd' means 'limited liability'.	Can be very large, e.g. the multinationals, with subsidiary private companies. 'l' of plc means 'limited liability'.	Most are very large, and all different, e.g. Post Office and BBC. 'Limited liability'. Many privatised by Conservatives 1979–97.

It is essential to understand 'LIMITED LIABILITY' (i.e. 'Ltd' or 'plc'). It is a warning – to whom? Stakeholders?

NB A **franchise** means a licence to use another business's name and products etc., so it is not a 'type of business' in the same sense. Less-expensive franchises (e.g. costing under £20,000) might be bought by sole traders or partnerships, while more costly franchises (e.g. a famous fast-food brand for £750,000) are likely to be bought by a Limited company. The (14th) National Westminster Bank survey of franchising found the sector to be worth £7 billion, and to be employing 270,000 people. The average total initial outlay for setting one up had risen (from £40,200 in 1996) to £42,800 in 1997.

Objectives

Success means the achievement of stated objectives. Individuals, businesses and governments, and other 'stakeholders' of a business, are likely to have different objectives, which may impinge on those of other groups.

Individuals

Examples of conflict between the objectives of two groups of stakeholders (see p. 8).

Everyone is unique, and in a unique situation – with particular thoughts and emotions. The nature of the work will be an important determinant of the quality of working life, but an individual's evaluation of a job could be influenced by several factors, e.g.

- fulfilling work/job satisfaction
- a good rate of pay
- long breaks and holidays
- lifestyle/combine work and family
- opportunities to be creative
- responsibility
- teamwork/friendship

- a valuable or interesting product
- good opportunities for promotion
- prestige/status
- job security
- a degree of independence
- recognition/praise.

Which of these means more to you – on a scale of one to five?

> *'Over half of spouses are met for the first time in the workplace!'*
> The Industrial Society (3/98).

Attitudes to work vary from finding work rewarding, with opportunities to use initiative, be creative, or express some other skill or talent, to feeling like part of the machinery, and alienated because of boring and repetitive work. Pay may be used as an incentive to make people work harder, but it cannot make them enjoy their work. Conditions of work vary, from workplaces which are air-conditioned, well-lit, brightly-decorated and with a pleasant working atmosphere, to others where temperature is not adequately controlled, fabric has deteriorated, and/or personal relationships discouraged. Research into **stress** at work has found that the way individuals are treated is a main feature of job satisfaction. Work is about feeling valued as well as gaining income.

Abraham Maslow identified 'The Hierarchy of Needs' (in 1970):

A useful base for analysis of what drives us humans, but unlikely as a topic (on its own) for an exam question.

Self-fulfilment	...self-actualisation
Ego	...responsibility, status
Belonging	...love, friendship
Safety	...security, shelter
Basic	...food, drink, warmth

Individuals try to satisfy these needs in a systematic manner, with the next particular set of needs affecting behaviour until they are satisfied, at which time the individual will move on up to the next level. The workplace is vital to achieving several of the needs:

- pay, perhaps with overtime or bonuses, can allow coverage of **basic needs**

- laws, e.g. on contracts, and unions, might affect **safety needs**

- teamwork and social facilities may help achieve **belonging needs**

- recognition, perhaps leading to promotion, could help on **ego needs**

- empowerment, share ownership schemes, or even self-employment might mean achievement of **self-fulfilment/self-actualisation**.

Criticisms: If a person cannot pay the rent (safety) then it may not matter whether they have status at work (ego) but Maslow's conclusions were that all people have the same needs and rank them in exactly the same order. Perhaps a person on a low income may still seek a status symbol (e.g. designer jeans?), even though some (basic) needs have not been achieved. Some individuals may not have the same need of security, esteem of others, or a need to belong to a group. Needs are affected by background, culture and current lifestyle.

But Maslow's theory, with its emphasis on the importance of an individual's higher-level needs being satisfied, can be used as a starting point for analysis of how people will behave in the workplace, with implications for Human Resource Management who have to take account of employees' personal objectives, particularly where they may conflict with those of the business (or the managers!) [see Topic 5 Human resource management, p. 34 Change].

Governments

How different are the objectives of the main political parties?

Political and social aims, e.g. winning votes/elections, reviewing the structure of the Welfare State, increasing Prison Service efficiency, or new laws on consumer protection, have economic consequences. The main economic aims can be summarised as:

- **Standard of living** – the main overall target, achieved by economic growth and usually measured by *Gross National Product (GNP) per capita*.

- **Prices** – a main target (since the 1970s) due to uncertainty created by inflation.

- **Employment** – e.g. high unemployment, once defined, may require action.

- **International trade** – e.g. a large and increasing net outflow of currency (shown in *the Balance of Payments Accounts*) may require policy action.

- **Distribution of income** – What is fair? e.g. Which individuals and businesses should pay more tax or receive more of state expenditure, e.g. grants?

Before the 1997 election Tony Blair said there were three priorities when they had won the election: 'Education, education ...and education'! [see Topic 7 Operations management, p. 73 Location and p. 88 Kaizen].

Businesses will be affected by the economic objectives and subsequent policy decisions of a government [see Topic 10 External influences], e.g:

- A cutback on spending on roads will mean fewer contracts for businesses.

- A Budget change to the rate of Corporation Tax affects business profits.

- The raising of interest rates make business loans more costly.

What about the business you are considering, e.g. for an exam case study?

Businesses

Maximum profit might be the obvious objective for every business, but depending on the business itself and its situation [see Topic 10 External influences], there are various other possibilities:

- maximise profit
- increase market share
- survival – e.g. in a recession
- to go public – e.g. to raise capital
- research and develop new products
- improve quality
- maximise sales revenue

- improve efficiency/reduce costs
- growth/expansion
- diversification
- launch a new product successfully
- to operate ethically
- to provide a public service – e.g. in the public sector.

Objectives may have to be changed, in response to a changing organisation and the economic climate. Directors of larger organisations may issue a **mission statement**, outlining longer-term objectives and the way it is hoped the organisation will operate. **Ethics** issues may be addressed, recognising a need, in very competitive markets, to present the right image to stakeholders, e.g. an oil company's customers and shareholders, and also Greenpeace.

> 'We are living in an area of corporate self-doubt. In the 80s aims were pure, easily identified and uttered without shame or qualification: the principal aim was to make money. Profits were praised. Shareholders ruled.
> Now, the unbridled pursuit of profits (or more accurately earnings per share) is considered slightly vulgar. There must be more to running a company...Hence, the increasing use of the fashionable phrase "stakeholders", usually taken to mean a wide group of organisations and individuals who interrelate with a company.'
>
> The Guardian (10/10/92).

Management by objectives (MBO)

- Setting objectives for workers, and having regular follow-up meetings.
- Aims to enhance motivation, assessment/appraisal and training.
- Objectives can be maintained or revised – higher or lower, at next meeting.
- Widely used by managers to improve performance.
- Proposed by Peter Drucker, in *The Practice of Management* (1954).

Useful for planning exams – modular or linear?

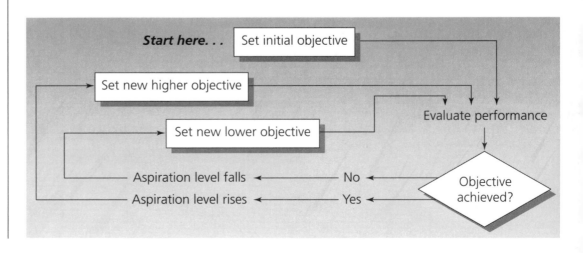

Advantages:

- managers have continual encouragement to plan
- individuals know what is expected, and self-development encouraged
- regular involvement of the workers may encourage their commitment
- individuals' objectives more easily integrated within the organisation's
- regular reviews encouraging better communication and feedback
- improvements to appraisal of staff and processes, and more objective
- clarifies the structure of the organisation and the roles of personnel.

Disadvantages:

- considerable time and effort required
- commitment and co-ordination from every tier required
- changes in the structure, management styles and control procedures required
- possible management frustration because of dependence on more personnel
- setting specific goals may reduce creativity and encourage conservatism
- *'short-termism'* may be encouraged, at the expense of long-term goals
- may still be seen as a method of control by managers.

Aims – longer-term general goals of the organisation, often unquantifiable and qualitative, e.g. to maximise profits, or growth, or market share.

Objectives – longer-term specific goals, which should be quantifiable, e.g. to achieve a certain percentage growth per annum, or particular fraction share of the market.

Organisation

Organisational charts

Try to use business examples rather than your own organisation.

- Show locations – of individuals, jobs or departments within the hierarchy, based on specialisations, locations, products or customers.

- Confirm roles – questions of accountability, of each department and individual, may be easier to resolve, e.g. for new employees.

- Show lines of communication – horizontal and vertical, focusing management attention on reducing barriers to effective communication, e.g. feedback both ways.

But they:

- may only be applicable for a short time, where an organisation is dynamic and constantly changing.

- do not show informal relationships, including groups, although these may be important influences on behaviour within an organisation. Relationships may well be more complex than shown, especially where responsibilities not clearly allocated.

An 'upside-down' organisational chart can be drawn, to show managers as supporters or facilitators of those who interface with customers. Should the shareholders be included in a chart for a limited company? Does their exclusion illustrate 'the divorce of ownership from control'?

Chain of command

This is the line of authority running from the top of the management hierarchy to the grass roots/shop-floor/lowest-rank employees.
Better-educated and trained specialist managers have led to more tiers in most management hierarchies, and thus longer chains of command. The Armed Services and the Police have clear examples:

The length of the chain will depend on several factors:

- size of the organisation
- extent of diversification
- controls required – how complex?

- the product – how complex?
- geographical spread
- type of people employed – supervise?

Many large businesses turn divisions into subsidiaries, with their own shorter chains of command. Younger managers with potential can be given earlier opportunities for promotion, to motivate them, and discourage them from being poached by a competing organisation in the market.

Name four large Japanese car companies [see Topic 7 Operations management, p. 85 JIT].

1994/5: Ford Motor Corporation (US) reduced the number of tiers in its management hierarchy from 14 to 7. The main reasons for the 'delayering' were to:

- Reduce wage costs to be competitive, particularly against the large Japanese multinational car producers. Short-term costs were higher, due to increased administration costs and redundancy payments (where natural wastage insufficient).

- Improve communication, through fewer tiers, allowing more effective decision-making, with less time and costs involved.

Span of control

This is the number of subordinates reporting directly to a particular manager.

An organisation will have a flatter (horizontal) hierarchy, with fewer tiers, if it is assumed that managers can effectively manage a large span/number of subordinates.

A taller (vertical) hierarchy, with more management tiers, would be set up if it is believed superiors can only effectively manage a small span/number of subordinates.

Henri Fayol [see Topic 5 Human resource management, p. 23 Motivation] proposed that a narrow span, between three and six, was ideal for most organisations.

Advantages:
- tighter control
- better co-ordination
- reduced delegation
- easier communication
- managers with more time to think and plan.

Disadvantages:
- more time taken up, if less decision-making authority for subordinates
- less motivation of them
- greater supervisory costs.

Modern research suggests there is no one ideal span, but that it depends on:
- the complexity of the work, in terms of its depth and breadth
- the variety of the work
- quality of management – ability, skills and experience
- quality of subordinates, in terms of ability, skills and experience
- the technology involved – new?
- the general stability of the organisation – can risks be taken?

Centralisation and decentralisation

Many large businesses are highly centralised, e.g. large food retailers involved in 'Store Wars', with major policy decisions taken at HQ.

Advantages of **centralised organisations:**
- control of the organisation by the directors can be more direct
- uniformity, e.g. in quality and merchandising, can be achieved
- experts, if correct, are most effectively used on a large scale
- economies of scale can be increased further, e.g. bulk-buying of stock.

Advantages of **decentralised organisations:**
- motivation may be enhanced by more local involvement and discretion
- initiative could be more forthcoming from workers at local level
- local market differences could be better understood
- local decisions could be made more quickly, as required.

Two types of organisational chart.

Apply these to a case.

Name five businesses in 'Store Wars'. Which one led with 15% of the market in 1998?

Management and leadership

All organisations require managing because they are constantly having to change, at least to some extent, so managers need to make decisions [see Topic 8 Data and information technology, p. 93 Decision trees]. Whether it is for production of beer or vehicles, farming or banking, the same kinds of decisions have to be taken, including:

- what to produce
- how to produce it
- how much to produce
- how much to charge   and...

- when to produce it
- where to produce it
- for whom to produce
- whether to produce at all.

Henry Mintzberg, in *The Nature of Managerial Work* (1973), concluded that decision-making was the most important function of managers:

- **Entrepreneur** decisions, on manager's own initiative, to take advantage of a changing economic environment, e.g. diversification into another country.

- **Disturbance handler** decisions, reacting to events beyond the manager's control, e.g. in another department of the business, or in the market or the economy.

- **Negotiator** decisions, when a manager is dealing with several types of people, including superiors and subordinates in the hierarchy, suppliers and customers.

- **Resource allocator** decisions on how all the various assets/resources are to be used, including scheduling time, programming work and authorising action.

Worth mentioning in an exam answer on 'management'.

Economists distinguish between four factors of production:

- land – includes land resources, but also the sea (e.g. for trawling or oil exploration) and fresh water (e.g. for hydro-electric power or fish-farming)

- labour – all the different types of workers and skills needed for production of the particular good or service

- capital – in the form of buildings, plant and machinery, or money available for investment by the organisation

- entrepreneur – the risk-taking function of managers, which involves setting objectives.

N.B. 'land' includes water!

Business managers would split their organisation's resources down into more categories, usually allocated to different departments. Changes could be minor (e.g. switching to a similar raw material) or major (e.g. loss of key personnel), resulting from internal factors, or from a changing business environment.

Not to scale!

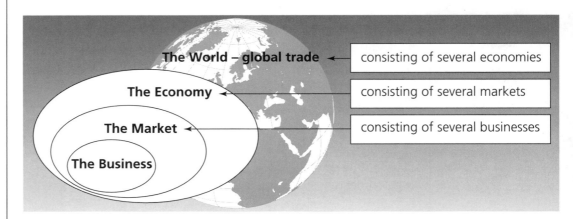

The World – global trade	consisting of several economies
The Economy	consisting of several markets
The Market	consisting of several businesses
The Business	

Ex-Chairman
of ICI plc and 'The
Troubleshooter' on
BBC Television.

'Without question, the most desirable management skill for the '90s will be the ability to manage change...Management has always been about change, for it is, uniquely, the task of making more, or better, from less...The Learning Company is one that continually changes.'

Sir John Harvey-Jones, *Managing to Survive* (1993).

SWOT analysis

This is necessary for assessing current and future possible market situations of the business.

- **Strengths** – e.g. the business is well-established, with an encouraging market share, and management have detailed knowledge of the market.

- **Weaknesses** – e.g. the business is well-established, but is product-led and management seems unwilling to change, to remain competitive.

- **Opportunities** – e.g. to diversify into a related or completely different, new product and/or into another country, perhaps also in the Single Market.

- **Threats** – e.g. from foreign businesses likely to increase the competition in the domestic market for the products of the business.

May be well worth
doing for a case study
business, e.g. for a
modular exam.

S and W are
'current'.
O and T are
'potential'.

PEST analysis

This is used to facilitate analysis of the overall environment of a business [see Topic 10 External influences].

- **Political** – including government (and opposition?) policies, legislation, European Union (EU) directives and regulations, action by pressure groups.

- **Economic** – including current trends for economic growth, inflation, unemployment, interest rates and exchange rates.

- **Social** – including demographic, social and cultural trends.

- **Technological** – including new products, processes and materials, as well as developments in Information Technology (IT).

Rising expectations of consumers could be a crucial aspect.

How would the workers in a business be affected?

Change is inevitable: the problem is how best to harness that change and use its consequences for the benefit of the organisation.

A famous
American
management
guru.

'We don't have to wait for the future: we can shape it, but there isn't much time.'

Charles Handy, *The Changing Worlds of Organisations* (1995).

Managerial styles

Robert Blake, with fellow organisational psychologist Jane Mouton, developed (Texas, 1961) a detailed **classification of managerial styles** based on the American post-war oil industry. **Blake's Grid** attempts to evaluate managers on 'concern for people' and 'concern for production':

Where would you appear on the grid?

Concern for people

High	**9**	1-9						9-9
	8							
	7							
	6							
	5				5-5			
	4							
	3							
	2							
Low	**1**	1-1						9-1
		Low						High

Concern for production

Leaders/managers can be given a rating, from one to nine, for each dimension. 'Concern for production' is the first rating in each case, e.g.

1-9 was described as 'country club' by Blake and Mouton, and indicates thoughtful attention to people's needs, a lack of conflict (beneficial?), and a comfortable friendly organisation atmosphere and work tempo.

9-9 indicates high productivity achieved by committed people, with a smooth integration of task and human requirements. Careful attention would be paid to 'ergonomics'.

5-5 represents middle-of-the-road management with attempts to improve productivity, but not with the workforce stretched to full capacity.

1-1 indicates that management are prepared to allow relatively poor production – quantity and/or quality, from demotivated workers.

9-1 style of leadership sometimes known as 'task management', i.e. getting the job done efficiently, but without consideration of workers' thoughts, attitudes and feelings.

Think of some famous, and not so famous examples – try and get four of each. Label them!

'Still going strong 30 years after it was developed, the Grid's unchanging purpose is to demonstrate, in special training courses, how leaders can modify their own management styles, become personally more effective, and develop the synergy in their teams...With companies demanding flatter structures with fewer middle management "facilitators" and more teamwork, the Grid's applications today could be endless.'

Management Today (3/91).

Modifications have been made to 'Blake's Grid', e.g. Dr Reddin's addition of 'effectiveness' as a third dimension.

Still used!

Case 1:

'A Harrods buyer who was driven out of her job for being too considerate towards staff in the two highly successful departments that she ran, won her case for constructive dismissal yesterday. Mrs C., 50, told the hearing in Croydon that she was forced out of her job last May because her approach towards staff was "not despotic" enough. Andrea Warden, her immediate superior, said the real reason for her demotion was that she was too soft. Mrs C. told the hearing: "Andrea told me the Harrods policy of treating their staff was to tread on their fingers. I thought I would do things differently and treat staff like friends."...Mrs C. was awarded the maximum compensation of £11,000 by an industrial tribunal.'

The Times (6/6/95).

Can you pick out the key aspects?

Case 2:

'A former Grenadier Guards drum major reduced staff to tears and lost business worth £500,000 when he brought his parade ground tactics to private industry, an industrial tribunal was told yesterday...Employed as area manager of a security firm in Luton, he once swore at a salesman and then frog-marched him by the elbow from an executive meeting. The incident proved too much for his employers and Mr H., 54, was sacked after 16 years' service. A director said that staff chose to take voluntary redundancy under a restructuring of the firm in 1993 rather than continue to work under Mr H.'s oppressive regime. The company had even sent him on a management "charm" course to try to rid him of his domineering style before he was eventually dismissed from his £25,000-a-year job.'

The Times (23/6/95).

The difference between a manager and a leader

Managers – responsible for setting objectives and using resources efficiently.

Leaders – motivate a group of people to use their individual skills and energies, so leadership could therefore be a key skill of a successful manager.

> *'A good manager can keep even an inefficient company running relatively smoothly, but a good leader can transform a demoralised organisation – whether it's a company, a football team or a nation...Whether you're the boss or a middle manager, you can benefit from improving your leadership skills. Leadership does not simply happen. It can only develop from experience, taking risks and learning from mistakes. Learn how to delegate and motivate; organise and chastise; praise and raise.'*
>
> Michael Shea, *Leadership Rules* (1993).

Leadership

The ability to persuade people to do things they would not do voluntarily.

There are several sources of a leader's ability to influence people's behaviour:

- **fear** – a manager may have the power to induce fear, e.g. a threat of disciplinary action

- **expertise** – this may give credibility and respect from others, e.g. in research

- **reward** – in a business the reward for co-operation might be the possibility of promotion

- **charisma** – this is the power of personality, as found in some religious sects, and politics.

Several different theories have been developed to explain the role of leadership, and to suggest 'best practice' of this fundamental aspect of management.

Dr Rensis Likert (1903–1981)

American industrial psychologist, carried out research (from the 1940s on) into improving the performance of human resources, to achieve good labour relations, higher productivity, and greater profitability. He concluded that the types of leadership throughout an organisation were crucial to its performance and there could be four types:

Think of a range of very different leaders from history – why did/do people follow their ideas?

A key figure for exam answers.

Again, consider some examples of leaders.

(i) Exploitative-authoritative

- Decisions imposed on subordinates.
- 'Stick' rather than 'carrot' used for motivation.
- Great responsibility for senior managers, but little for other workers.
- Relatively little communication.
- Little teamwork.

(ii) Benevolent-authoritative

- Condescending paternal influence, or master/servant trust.
- Mainly 'carrots' for motivation.
- Only managers have responsibility.
- Little communication.
- Little teamwork

(iii) Consultative

- Superiors have substantial, but not total, trust in subordinates.
- 'Carrots' and some involvement used to motivate.
- Relatively high proportion of workers feel responsible for achievement of the organisation's objectives.
- Some communication – vertical and horizontal.
- Some teamwork.

(iv) Participative

- Emphasis on group/teamwork.
- Superiors have complete confidence in ability of subordinates.
- Economic rewards/'carrots' based on agreed goals.
- Considerable communication – vertical and horizontal.

Likert concluded that type (iv) was ideal for a business with profit a main objective but also with a concern about the welfare of its human resources. For an effective participative leadership style:

Maintaining self-esteem is crucial in exam preparation too – how can you do that?

- employees must be treated as individuals, and self-esteem must be maintained or enhanced

- motivation must be by modern principles [see Topic 5 Human resource management, p. 22 Motivation] rather than by the traditional 'stick and carrot' methods

- teams of workers need to be built up, who are committed to the objectives of the organisation, with mutual respect to foster effectiveness.

Critics of Likert have pointed out examples in the 1980s and '90s of businesses dominated by one strong personality which have been able to respond very quickly to changes in the economic environment, e.g.

Find out about any you have not heard of.

Richard Branson, John DeLorean, Lord Hanson, Lee Iacocca, Robert Maxwell, Rupert Murdoch, Anita Roddick, and many others.

Professor James Clawson (of Charlottesville, Virginia)

Formulated the **VCM** Model of Leadership, in *Survey of Managerial Style* (1988) – a leader's personal profile will have three characteristics:
- vision
- commitment
- management skills.

One of three leadership styles would result:
- balanced – with roughly equal measures of the three characteristics
- visionary – with a clear bias towards forward-thinking
- managerial – with clear emphasis on the skills of management.

What *is* 'credibility'?

Kouses and Posner

Emphasised, in *Credibility: How Leaders Gain and Lose It, Why People Demand It* (1993) the importance of **credibility**, which is dependent on a leader's ability to:

- Discover him/herself – being clear in their own minds about values and standards, and being confident that they can deliver what they believe in.

- Appreciate followers – recognising that they are engaging in a relationship with followers which requires a deep understanding of what they, the followers, need. They must learn to listen – something managers are traditionally poor at.

- Affirm shared values – finding common ground to unite the organisation, but acknowledging the diversity of followers [see Topic 2 Objectives, p. 6 Individuals].

- Develop capacity – ensuring that those who follow have skills, knowledge and information to carry out their strategy by providing them with the appropriate training and development.

- Serve a purpose – recognising that they are the servants of the organisation and must embody their own standards and values in everything they do.

- Sustain hope – perhaps most importantly, inspiring enthusiasm and optimism.

Experts say it is also crucial for a student to maintain his or her self-esteem during preparation for exams.

Two extreme types of leadership

The Autocrat sets objectives, allocates tasks and demands obedience.

Advantages:
- the group will respond quickly
- direction will tend to be consistent.

Disadvantages:
- the group will be dependent on the leader and perhaps unable to operate without him/her – lack of information and/or cohesion
- constant supervision of the group will be required
- the group may become dissatisfied with the leader.

A direct comparison is often useful for exam answers. Use Likert as well.

The Democrat encourages participation in decision-making by consulting group members, delegating where possible, and explaining decisions.

Advantages:
- commitment of members to the group will be enhanced
- participation will be improved
- satisfaction of group members may rise
- quality of output will improve.

Disadvantages:
- heavy reliance on good communication skills
- respect for the leader may diminish.

Which type of leadership is more appropriate depends on:
- the task
- tradition and/or precedent
- type of group members
- leader's personality
- size of the group

- personalities of members
- amount of time available.

Delegation

Delegation is when a manager entrusts work to people lower down in the hierarchy.

So delegation may not be 'empowerment'.

In some cases less interesting tasks might simply be off-loaded onto a subordinate who would prefer not to have those responsibilities! Empowerment, a 1990s buzz-word in many large businesses, is the form of delegation where the individual, as well as the organisation, benefits from having the greater responsibility and authority, e.g. to halt the production line themselves, immediately, if they become aware of a quality problem.

Delegation can bring several possible benefits.

- It can motivate the subordinates who are delegated the tasks.
- It allows for the development of employees throughout the organisation.
- It breaks down the decision-making process and allows quicker decisions.

Evaluation, e.g. for high marks in an exam answer.

But there are also some possible problems.

- Subordinates may not be sufficiently skilled to undertake the tasks.
- The authority necessary to carry out the task may not go with the responsibility for it.
- Responsibility and/or authority may not be precisely defined.

Some managers may be reluctant to delegate authority because of a lack of confidence in subordinates, or because they are slow to realise the potential benefits. Also some leaders may wish to retain as much power/influence as possible within the organisation. Delegation involves a **calculated risk**.

Human resource management

When people go to work they take with them their personal background, influences, emotions, hopes, fears, results of many relationships, and their own objectives [see Topic 2 Objectives]. They are the only 'factor of production' that thinks, talks back, contributes to decision-making, and can vote with their feet (or have computers caught up yet?). Every individual is different, but he or she may belong to formal and informal groups with established norms.

After the Second World War, separate Personnel Departments were set up in larger businesses to perform the increased personnel functions:

- recruitment
- staff appraisal
- administering training and development
- staff welfare
- legislation affecting the workplace
- pay negotiations
- administering the payment scheme
- administering company pension scheme
- industrial relations.

Since the mid-1980s, there have been more advertisements for 'Human Resource Managers' rather than 'Personnel Managers'. Is there a difference?

NO: It is merely a name change designed to enhance the image and status (and salaries), of Personnel Managers.

YES: The job has changed, with increasing responsibilities, importance and status (and pay). HR Managers use more sophisticated techniques, e.g. in recruitment testing and staff development, and Human Resource Planning now usually has a more significant role in planning an overall business strategy.

Most jobs have disadvantages but workers will enjoy work if these can be minimised. Job satisfaction will be a complex mix including:

- the individual employee
- the groups/teams
- the job
- the business
- the rewards
- the working environment.

See both sides!

Groups

Most individuals spend very little time on their own, and most of the time in some type of group situation. A group can be defined as:

> *'a recognisable collection of people, organised formally or informally, whose inter-relationships are based on a range of identifiable characteristics'.*

Which groups do you belong to... voluntarily?

Where there is a well-defined common purpose, for example by management in a workplace, the group may be referred to as a team. Individuals are all unique products of

What is meant by 'synergy' (or '2 + 2 = 5')?

heredity and environment, with distinct personalities and complex and changing needs, but when they are in the workplace and come into contact with a group, they modify their behaviour to fit in with other workers and the needs of the job. Sociologists claim that a group norm, i.e. an acceptable code of behaviour will develop, and there are four types of groups:

- **Primary** – where members meet at frequent and regular intervals, e.g. the family, the one with the greatest long-term influence.
- **Secondary** – where members do not have daily or frequent contact with each other, e.g. managers of a large organisation, or members of a trade union, or club.
- **Informal** – where members join due to a common interest, e.g. for a type of music, hobby or sport. There would be no set rules for joining, or elected officials.
- **Formal** – where there are rules for membership, and officials to run them. They may have been deliberately set up as teams or departments within an organisation.

Managers need to be aware of both formal and informal groups that have formed in the workplace. Group tasks may need to be set, perhaps as part of Management-By-Objectives (MBO) [see Topic 2 Objectives], and it may be easier to motivate groups/teams of workers rather than individuals. Objectives of some informal groups may conflict with those of the organisation, creating a management problem. With an appreciation of group norms, and its power within the particular group, managers can influence the group so as to minimise possible conflict. Apparently, power *through* the group is far more effective in the longer term than power *over* the group.

Decision-making

A group decision is often more important and binding than an individual one. An individual can change his or her mind relatively easily, but it is often less easy for a committee to decide on a change in the course of action. The three stages to the decision-making process are:

- defining what the current task involves
- how the group will be organised
- how group members will work together.

Group effectiveness

'The best committee is a committee of one!'

There seem to be four main determinants of the effectiveness of a group:

- **The Leader** will have a given set of views about priorities and the course of action to be taken.
- **The Subordinates** will also have a given set of views, about how they should be led and what needs to be done. They will relate to tasks in different ways, with different levels of commitment.
- **The Task** will vary in nature, complexity, time scale and importance.
- **The Environment** will also vary, according to the nature of the group, the position of the manager in the group, the objectives of the group or organisation, and the structure and technology of the organisation.

Researchers Gilligan, Neale and Murray, in *Business Decision Making* (1983) identified 12 features leading to effective group performance:

1 The structure of the group and the status of the group members should be stable and well formed.

2 The group should be large enough to fulfil the tasks, but not so large as to encourage the formation of sub-groups.

3 The group members should have appropriate skills.

4 The atmosphere should be informal and relaxed.

5 Objectives should be understood and accepted by members.

6 Discussion should be encouraged and members willing to listen to each other.

7 Decisions should be reached by consensus.

8 The leader of the group should not dominate, nor should there be evidence of a struggle for power.

9 The group should operate with low/moderate stress levels.

10 Disagreements should not be overridden. Instead, the reasons for disagreement should be examined and an attempt made to resolve them.

11 Allocation of tasks to members should be clear and accepted.

12 The group should act in a cohesive way.

Communication

This will be affected by the formal and informal organisation of the group, and the means of communication. A. Bavelas in *A Mathematical Model for Group Structure* (1948) concluded there were four main types of communication network:

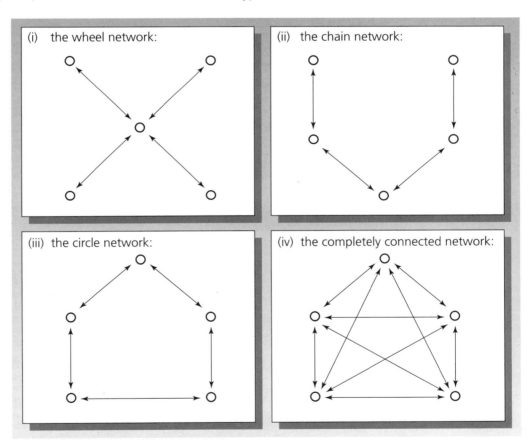

Bavelas noted that both the **wheel** and the **chain networks** are typified by a centralisation of the flow of information. Effective decision-making thus depends on those in key central positions and the quality of communications channels to them. He concluded that these two types of network were best suited to short-term operating control decisions. The **circle** and **completely connected networks** lend themselves to a more decentralised form of decision-making, where group members are mutually interdependent and share decision-making. Bavelas concluded that, in these cases, the group is less dependent on key individuals and levels of satisfaction are usually greater. Disadvantages might include some difficulty in pushing through decisions because responsibility is shared, and also talk about action will not necessarily provide the mechanism for it. Such open networks might be most suitable for periodic control and strategic decisions, where high-quality decisions need a substantial amount of discussion and shared analysis and evaluation. However long-term and major policy decisions will also require leadership, perhaps from a leader who can say *'the buck stops here'*.

Are groups more effective at decision-making than individuals?

What does your experience suggest?

It depends on the context, but usually the quality of a group's decision-making will be higher because of the quantity and quality of data that can be included in the considerations [see Topic 3 Organisation, p. 11 Span of control]. Perhaps, for a small group, five members is ideal because:

- the odd number will prevent an impasse
- the group is large enough to take in several different opinions, and perhaps to avoid mistakes resulting from the power of an individual with an entrenched view
- everyone can be involved.

Motivation

What motivates you, e.g. in your studies?

In the latter half of the 19th century, the population grew rapidly, just as the Reverend T. R. Malthus had predicted in *Essay on Population* (1798). It provided a larger workforce, and larger markets for food and manufactured goods, in several European economies. The growing banking system, with new laws allowing further development of 'limited liability', made larger quantities of capital available for investment by businesses. These expanded, but so did the competition in most markets.

By the end of the 19th century there was a clear need for managers to achieve **competitiveness** by increasing efficiency of production, but this task was hampered by growing conflict between the requirements of management, on behalf of owners, and the aspirations of other workers, [see Topic 2 Objectives]. Motivation of the workforce became an important focus for business people, psychologists and sociologists.

Main theories

Frederick W. Taylor (1865–1915)

What motivates a professional musician, or sportsman or woman?

- Formulated 'Scientific Management' – an objective approach to management problems, based on observing and measuring rather than subjective judgements.
- Rose from apprentice steel machinist to Chief Engineer (with evening classes to get his engineering degree).
- Consultant to several steel companies, and Henry Ford – to improve production of the 'Model T' at the huge River Rouge plant in Detroit.
- Invention of high-speed steel cutting tools allowed him to retire aged 45, and he spent the rest of his life lecturing (unpaid) to promote 'scientific management'.
- He emphasised **increasing efficiency of production** – to reduce costs and enhance profits, but also so workers would benefit from increased earnings.
- Increased productivity could be attained with no extra human energy being required, via 'scientific management'.
- The main job of managers was selection and training of workers and, because most individuals would see work as unpleasant, pay is the main motivator.

> *'The principal object of management should be to secure the maximum prosperity for the employer, coupled with the maximum prosperity of each employee.'*
>
> F. W. Taylor

The main effects of Taylor's theories:

Why was the word scientific used, then?

- Emphasis on productivity at shop floor level has led to many modern management techniques, e.g. standard costing and work study [see Topic 7 Operations management].

- Emphasis on pay as the prime motivator led to widespread use of piece rates and bonuses, based on norms established by time studies.

- Many workers felt threatened by the new techniques of 'scientific management' and began to organise themselves more effectively. Taylor's ideas were held to be partly responsible for the rise of American trade unions evident after early 1900s.

- Many employers gave 'scientific management', or 'Taylorism', a poor reputation, using the techniques as an excuse to extract greater productivity, and profit, from workers but without giving a commensurate increase in wages.

Henri Fayol (1841–1925)

- Emphasised the importance of taking a wider view, i.e. the organisation as a whole (rather than with Taylor's emphasis on shop floor management), but the analytical approach was similar.

- Managing Director of a large coal mining company, he analysed his and other businesses for methods of achieving **optimum performance**.

- He divided industrial (primary or secondary) production into six activities:
  - technical (production)
  - organisation (material and human structures)
  - financial (optimum use of capital)
  - security (protection of property and persons)
  - accounting (including statistics)
  - managerial.

Choose four or five for your revision notes.

- He divided management into five elements: [see Topic 4 Management and leadership]
  - foresight (forecasting and planning)
  - organisation (material and human structures)
  - command (maintenance of activity)
  - co-ordination
  - control.

- He went on to list 14 principles of management:

  1 Division of work – opportunities for increased efficiency through specialisation.

  2 Authority and responsibility – to be related, for management to be effective.

  3 Discipline – effective discipline requires good managers at all levels.

  4 Unity of command – employers should receive orders from only one superior.

  5 Unity of direction – each organisational unit should have a single objective.

  6 Subordination of individual to general interest – 'goal congruence' essential.

  7 Fair remuneration – from both employer's and the employee's points of view.

  8 Centralisation – depending on the particular organisation and circumstances.

  9 The scalar chain – the chain of command to be followed, with rare exception.

  10 Order – every person and other resource to have an assigned place.

  11 Equity – all personnel within the company to be treated fairly.

12 Stability of tenure – job security to be provided wherever practicable.

13 Initiative – to be encouraged from subordinates, by managers.

14 *Esprit de corps* – teamwork and sound communications vital, to maintain the motivation of the workforce and management.

- Though some of the language now seems out of date, this list still applies to modern businesses.

Elton Mayo

Groups!

- American psychologist who founded the Human Relations School of Management.

- Led the Hawthorne Studies (1924–32) – a detailed study of worker behaviour carried out at the Western Electric Company's factory at Hawthorne, Chicago, requested because production was well below the factory's potential capacity.

- Experiments were done with groups of comparably performing workers, with levels of heating and lighting varied. Output of one group of female workers rose anyway, apparently because (from interviews) they were the focus of attention and felt united in a common aim. **Group morale** and a sense of participation overcame poor conditions.

- During the experiments, **group norms** were apparent, and important for how each group performed.

- Other research included interviewing of 20,000 workers (1928–30). Comments were asked for on working conditions, supervision and jobs in Western Electric, and on 'any other problems'.

- Results of this research led Mayo to conclude that pay and good working conditions were not the main motivators of most workers. More important were:
  - the nature of the job
  - types of supervision and leadership
  - and, particularly, relationships affecting group morale.

Douglas McGregor

- American management consultant.

- Supported (Mayo's) Human Relations School.

- Wrote *The Human Side of Management* (1960), emphasising **management theory and employee motivation** – he compared traditional management philosophy of direction and control (which some people equated with 'Taylorism') with a more modern approach of encouraging job satisfaction and trying to lift the human spirit.

- **'Theory X'** – the management style of organising, directing and controlling workers, using 'sticks and carrots' to get the planned work done, assuming that most individuals:
  - dislike work
  - avoid work
  - are lazy and selfish
  - have to be directed, controlled and/or threatened
  - avoid responsibility
  - have little ambition
  - are motivated purely by money.

Taylor unfairly blamed? Best not to have 'McGregor versus Taylor' in an answer.

- **'Theory Y'** – a more modern and enlightened management style, where managers would allow workers to have responsibility and display initiative, because individuals:
  - find work satisfying
  - seek work
  - work well, and co-operate
  - are self-directed/motivated

- seek responsibility
- seek satisfaction of higher needs
- are motivated by all the needs.

Abraham Maslow (1908–1970)

- American psychology professor, famous for formulating **'The Hierarchy of Needs'** – part of his analysis of what drives people, especially how they derive motivation in the workplace [see Topic 2 Objectives].

- The hierarchy resembles a person's ordinary lifecycle, with a self-motivating adult finally emerging. Needs would disappear as they were satisfied, e.g. an individual gaining a new job would soon forget the initial pleasure and move on to seeking promotion, status or recognition.

- But, if these needs were not achieved, the individual might be just as dissatisfied as they were before they got a new job. He emphasised that preventing the satisfying of a need could only be done by a force outside the individual, e.g. management in the workplace.

Frederick Herzberg

Hertzberg in some books.

- American psychology professor, whose research was seen as complementing Maslow's.

- Wrote *Work and the Nature of Man* (1966).

- His research involved questionnaires (to accountants and engineers) that asked what people thought about their jobs. Subsequent research has tended to confirm his findings.

- Two types of factors in the workplace – those that caused satisfaction, often leading to genuine motivation, seemed to be different to those which caused dissatisfaction – important implications for the managers responsible.

(a) Hygiene (or maintenance) factors contribute to avoidance of dissatisfaction:

A key aspect sometimes featuring in an exam question.

- security and fair treatment
- working conditions
- status
- management/supervision
- working relationships
- company policy and administration
- relative pay/wage/salary.

These need to be kept up or maintained at certain levels if performance, morale and motivation are not to reduce. Symptoms could be absenteeism, lower productivity and production, resistance to change, and negative work practices, e.g. obstructing the management in some way.

(b) Motivating factors contribute to worker satisfaction:

- psychological growth or 'self-actualisation'
- responsibility
- the work itself
- prospects for promotion
- recognition.

He recommended that a range of these should be built into the work situation, to bring about improvements to performance and motivation, and suggested three particular methods of incorporating them:

- **Job enrichment** involves an employee taking on more responsibility for their own work, with the necessary authority to decide how best to achieve desired results.

Know the difference!

Contrast with Taylor's view.

- **Job enlargement** would involve widening the training of the employee, to cover a wider range of tasks that they can perform, although still at the same level of skill.

- **Job rotation** would involve moving group members between the various tasks involved in their part of the production process, on a planned basis [see Topic 7 Operations management, p. 88 Quality Circles].

> *'If you want people motivated to do a good job, give them a good job to do.'*
> Frederick Herzberg

C. P. Alderfer

- Also developed (in the 1950s) a **needs-based theory**, similar to Maslow's but with only three levels:
  existence needs – similar to the two lower levels on Maslow's 'hierarchy of needs', and relate to physical comfort and survival
  relatedness needs – concerned with love, affiliation and belonging
  growth needs – concerned with self-development, independence and creativity.

- His **ERG Theory**, differed from Maslow's in that it emphasised that a lack of ability to satisfy higher-level needs might make lower-level needs even more important. Also he did not believe that lower-level needs had to be satisfied before higher-level needs could become motivators.

V. H. Vroom

Easy name to remember!

- Formulated 'Expectancy Theory' (in the 1960s).

- An individual's wants are related to the expectancy of being able to meet them.

Includes two factors or points of emphasis.

- **'Valencies'** are a measure of the want – high or low? If a high valence for a particular target is to act as a motivator, the individual concerned must believe that the target is attainable.

i.e. the final 'ripple' effect greater than the initial input(s).

- He used a diagram to illustrate the 'multiplier effect' of the **valence** (giving the level of importance attached to the want) and the **expectancy** (of attaining that want):

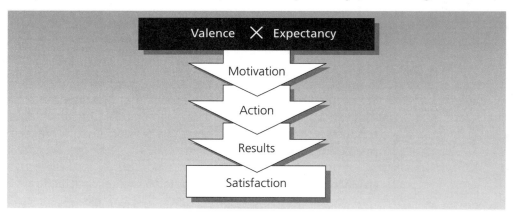

- The main implication is that working life should offer opportunities for workers' wants to be met, and provide clear evidence that targets are attainable.

W. Edwards Deming (1900–1993)

Revise in a very quiet, soft American accent. His followers hung on to every word!

- An American government statistician, who spent over 60 years developing a management philosophy which helped Japanese businesses like Toyota rebuild after the Second World War.

- He emphasised that a business using data to develop efficient systems, and management practices to ensure well-motivated workers, could improve both productivity and quality – according to the principle of *kaizen* [see Topic 7 Operations management, p. 88 Kaizen].

- Decorated by Emperor Hirohito in 1960, he would not become famous in his own country, and then in Europe, until the 1980s.

- He was still lecturing (usually for free, like Frederick Taylor) right up to his death, with an overall message that businesses should have highly systematic management but a style that values people highly.

> *'85% of a company's problems originate in bad management.'*
>
> *'Co-operation, not competition, is what made America great.'*
>
> Dr W. E. Deming

David McCelland

- Emphasised (also in the 1970s) the importance of achievement in the analysis of workers' motivation. His research suggested that every individual needs opportunities and experiences to be successful, and these should be provided wherever possible in the workplace.

E. H. Schein

- Classified **motivation theories** on motivation in the workplace, according to how each theory explains what drives human beings (again in the 1970s).

- Theories of motivation assume one of three types of human drives:
  - **Socio-economic drive** – people are driven by material urges, and satisfaction can be created by meeting these basic needs in the workplace.
  - **Social drive** – people have a basic need to feel part of a group, and to be accepted.
  - **Complex drive** – a broader perspective, with different factors changing over time and according to circumstances, avoiding simplistic explanations of motivation.

William Ouchi

- Published *Theory Z: How American Business Can Meet the Japanese Challenge* (New York, 1981).

- **'Theory Z'** was formulated to go alongside *'Theories X and Y'* [see McGregor], at a time when Japanese companies were gaining significant market shares in several industrial and consumer goods – with an edge in productivity and quality.

- Dr Ouchi claimed the source of their success lay in **HRM practices**.

- 'Theory Z', mainly based on Japanese practices, stressed the benefits of:
  - long-term employment – even in recession
  - slow evaluation and promotion – building up expertise and trust
  - multi-profession career paths, to avoid workers becoming less flexible
  - a mixture of *implicit* (built-in/understood) and *explicit* (added/stated) *control systems*
  - collective, participative decision-making/leadership [see Topic 4 Management and leadership] but with individual responsibility – favoured by most Western firms
  - 'holistic orientation', basically company concern for the overall employee welfare.

- Overall emphasis on motivation and teamwork, e.g. 'quality circles'.

> *'Mid-morning and the klaxon goes. Piped music starts to play, the car production lines stop and men walk away for their break. All work ceases until, ten minutes later, the hooter blares again and the lines start to roll. This is not Britain but a Toyota factory in Japan. The break is used not just for refreshment, but for corporate motivation and team-spirit building.'*
>
> The Times (20/1/93).

SSC!

Another easy name to remember?

Links well with an explanation of Japanese product techniques.

Up-to-date!
('M' is for
Manchester).

Can you think of
others, e.g. within
your organisation?

Why not choose five
of these 13 experts
for your final
revision notes?

Can you see
both sides?

Ivan Robertson

- Professor of Occupational Psychology (at UMIST).
- Published *Motivation: Strategies, Theory and Practice* (1993).
- Refutes optimistic theories that workers all become well-motivated if jobs are well designed, and they are 'enriched' by suitable challenges (see Herzberg!).
- There are *no* **universal motivators**.
- There *are* several possible **universal demotivators**, including:
  - giving the workforce no feedback about the effects of their efforts on output
  - giving the workforce feedback information but in an unclear form, so links between effort and rewards appear entirely random
  - contradictory or even vague work-goals [see Topic 2 Objectives, p. 8 Management by objectives].
  - targets imposed from on high without explanation, let alone consultation
  - arbitrary controls, e.g. a manager responding to an obviously isolated incident by overreacting and punishing everybody.

'Once you think about ways of turning everyone off, you suddenly realise what an awful lot of managers use them.'

Professor I. Robertson

Is pay the main motivator?

Levels of pay are certainly important to:
- Governments – perhaps concerned that wage inflation may drive up the overall inflation rate [see Topic 10 External influences].
- Individuals – whose pay is the main source of income, so determining their standard of living.
- Businesses – for which pay is a, or the, major cost of production, particularly if production is labour-intensive.

A management view

Pay should:
- help recruitment of the right quantity and quality of labour
- slow labour turnover, where recruitment and retraining costs are high
- hold down labour costs, to ensure competitiveness of the business
- encourage the workforce to be flexible, e.g. with no demarcation
- be part of an overall package, e.g. with fringe benefits and/or a share scheme
- motivate, towards maximum worker productivity.

A union view

Pay should:
- increase members' real earnings
- be part of a supportive environment, e.g. industrial relations, health and safety, and ergonomics
- take account of hours worked, breaks and holidays
- have bonuses based only on attainable targets
- provide longer-term benefits to members, e.g. with a share scheme
- encourage recognition of individuals' efforts and feedback to them
- motivate, towards job satisfaction.

The ideal pay system will vary according to:

- type of business – e.g. who is making crucial decisions
- type of work – e.g. dangerous, or output difficult to measure precisely
- size of the business – e.g. economies of scale reducing other unit costs
- types of employees – e.g. a risk of them being poached
- technologies used – e.g. particular safety and/or skills required
- time available for production – e.g. production highly seasonal
- the particular market – e.g. product the height of fashion.

Frederick Taylor's research and experience led him to conclude that, in most work situations, pay *is* the main determinant of level of motivation.

- Other possible motivators besides the basic rate of pay include:
  - comparative pay – compared to that of people doing similar work ('relativities') or with different skills or qualifications ('differentials')
  - security of employment – particularly in times of recession and high unemployment nationally, regionally or locally
  - status or promotion prospects – may compensate for pay not being high
  - job satisfaction – from interesting and challenging work may compensate
  - appraisal – with a supportive monitoring system, with feedback both ways
  - education and/or training – paid for by the business, for self-development
  - group acceptance – perhaps a priority [see Mayo's 'Hawthorne Studies'].

A useful list for an exam question starting, 'Besides pay ...'.

Human resource planning

[RAT]

(a) **Recruitment** – employing the right number of people, with the right skills and ability, at the right time.

(b) **Appraisal** – assessing employees' performance now, and how it might be improved, for future requirements.

(c) **Training** – development of methods for improving worker productivity and job satisfaction, via self-development.

(a) Recruitment

Some large businesses employ a specialist recruitment agency, e.g. for 'headhunting' a particularly suitable candidate for a vacancy. Otherwise, the Personnel or H. R. Department would consult with the department with the vacancy, and get the procedure in motion.

Job analysis – to identify the job's component parts and how it is performed:

- task analysis – to identify the exact component parts of the job in question
- activity analysis – dividing the task into physical (e.g. lifting) and mental
- skills analysis – using a 'skills audit' of the current workforce, e.g. the ability to work as part of a group/team [see p. 19 Groups], work independently, perform manual operations, communicate effectively, or follow instructions.

List the stages in your own revision notes.

Job description – a broad statement of the purpose, scope, duties and responsibilities, including:

- the title of the job
- to whom the employee is responsible
- for whom the employee is responsible
- a simple description of their relevant role and duties.

It will set the post in its context within the hierarchy of the organisation, and could be used as a job indicator for applicants for a job, or a guideline for an employee and/or the manager in charge.

Job specification – a more detailed version of what the job entails, used to decide the qualities and qualifications required of applicants.

Recruitment profile – listing the qualities of the ideal candidate, perhaps using 'The Seven Point Plan' devised by Alec Rodgers of the National Institute of Industrial Psychologists:

- Physical make-up – health, appearance, manner
- Attainments – experience and education
- General intelligence – ability to grasp problems quickly
- Special aptitudes – manual, verbal or numerical
- Interests – any relevant hobbies (reflecting personality?)
- Disposition – sociability, sense of responsibility and leadership
- Personal circumstances – the job's likely effects on private life, and vice versa.

The technique is similar to the photofit picture/software used by the police to identify likely culprits, on the basis of all information available at the time.

Have you started compiling your own c.v. yet? ... as part of marketing yourself in the future.

Job advertisement – which people will be targeted – internal and/or external candidates? Where should the advertisement be placed – in a trade journal?

An application form may be supplied to those people who respond to the advertisement. They may be asked to (hand-?)write a letter of application and enclose a curriculum vitae (c.v.), i.e. details of current and past employment, other relevant experience and qualifications, and the names of two referees (who can give opinions on the person's suitability for the job).

> 'Even 20 years ago, having the right connections and background helped bright young things secure a job in the City... Recruitment has now become a more rigorous and objective process, initiated via an application form (once rare but now issued by the vast majority of City institutions) and using psychometric testing [to test logic and reasoning skills], team exercises and presentations, alongside traditional interviews.'
>
> Sophie Hanscombe, Managing Editor of 'Human Resources Magazine', The Sunday Times (11/11/97).

As for gaining a place at university?

Candidates may be shortlisted for the post and invited for interview. The successful candidate will receive a letter of appointment, and (within 13 weeks of starting) should then be given a Contract of Employment to check and sign [see p. 48 The Law].

Recruit from within?

Advantages:

Can an interview say more about the interviewer than the interviewee?

- cost savings – on induction and further training
- less disruption – if they are already used to working with other employees, in a group/team [see p. 19 Groups]
- motivation – of existing employees encouraged by promotion possibilities
- less risky – their strengths and weaknesses already assessed [see p. 31 Appraisal].

Disadvantages:

- replacement – of the promoted candidate could create complications
- less 'objective' criticism of current practices, compared to that from an external appointee
- promotion – of a particular internal candidate may upset and demotivate some other existing employees.

(b) Appraisal

How is your academic (and sporting) performance appraised? How could it be more 'effective'?

In competitive markets where businesses are searching for ways of improving their performance, there will be a need to keep an asset register, and review staff performance systematically:

- to identify employee weaknesses
- to identify employee strengths
- to determine salary increases
- to determine who deserves promotion
- to improve internal communications
- to make decisions on staff training and development.

> *'Performance appraisal too often tends to be treated as a compulsory but indifferently maintained record system.'*
>
> Michael Williams, *Performance Appraisal in Management* (1972).

Effective appraisal systems can improve the performance of the individual for their own benefit, satisfaction and fulfilment of needs [see Topic 2 Objectives, p. 6 Maslow], as well as the organisation's.

Methods of appraisal

- Grading – employees given an overall grade, e.g. poor, average, etc.
- Ranking – a manager ranks subordinates in order of merit.
- Rating – employees are given points on a rating scale, e.g. 0–5, for each of a predetermined list of tasks and objectives
- Strengths and weaknesses – the appraiser makes lists of these, and may discuss these with the appraisee. Personal development, training and promotion prospects may then be discussed with the appraisee.
- Interview – the subordinate is encouraged to talk about successes and failures in the appraisal period, before discussion of how to improve performance in the future period. This method can be used on its own or with others.
- Self-appraisal – of the appraisee's own strengths and weaknesses, on a special form. Individual workers may see benefits of the exercise over a period of time, but it is often found to be a difficult task.

Who should do the appraising? Some organisations give appraisees some choice, e.g. for a negative preference, i.e. *not* to be appraised by a particular superior/manager, but usually the immediate superior will carry it out.

Following the appraisal, the appraiser and appraisee draw up an action plan as a basis for the next appraisal session. A successful system, that brings benefits to the employees and the organisation, requires commitment from both parties involved, over a period of time.

Evaluation! Consider both types of effects.

What do you think should be the objectives of a secondary school?

Training is 'a problem' in the UK.

Appraisal is an inexact process. Is it there to:

- check up on employees?
  or
- bring out the best in them?

(c) Training

The Department for Education and Employment's official (1971) definition of 'training':

> 'The systematic development of the attitude/knowledge/skill behaviour pattern required by an individual in order to perform adequately a given task or job.'

'Education' is different – usually said to be mind-broadening, not task- or job-specific, and valued for its own sake, not for its practical uses.

> 'The continual linking of Education to economic welfare is the sound of barbarism. Like all things joyous, beautiful and good, education is self-self-justified. It actually shrivels at the touch of secondary justification.'
>
> Enoch Powell MP (1985).

> 'At the heart of our reforms is the determination to break down the artificial barrier which for far too long divided an academic education from a vocational one.'
>
> PM John Major (1991).

In 1995 the Conservative Government merged the government departments for Education and Employment, apparently responding to claims from big businesses that education was not fitting out individuals for the world of work, and concerned with Britain slipping further down the international league table of competitiveness (from being 'The Workshop of the World' in the 1920s).

> 'For the average organisation, training [in 1995] amounts to 3.66% of the salary bill or an average of 0.85% of annual turnover – compared with 0.74% of turnover in 1993. It is the public/voluntary sector (average 1.07%) which spends the highest percentage of turnover on training, followed by the financial sector (0.9%), and the service sector spends the lowest (0.69%).'
>
> The Industrial Society's Briefing Plus (9/95).

In 1985 the government launched GNVQs (to be work-related equivalents of A levels) and NVQs (to be less academic training qualifications). In 1992 the government financed an initiative, called 'Investors in People' to encourage businesses to spend more on training. It takes the form of an award to organisations which have satisfied inspectors of a commitment in four areas:

- a system covering all employees
- a regular review of training needs
- development of individuals throughout their employment with the organisation
- evaluation of the effectiveness of the investment in training employees.

> 'The key issue is the avoidance of sticking-plaster training that puts in a system which brings together all the elements. If you have an appraisal system, this is not sufficient evidence alone for "Investors in People". The system must start from the objectives and where the company is going. It must focus on business as well as individual needs.'
>
> The Industrial Society supporting IIP, February 1994.

Successful organisations can use the 'Investor in People' statement in their marketing as a form of training standards 'kite-mark'. By February 1994 there were 5,000 organisations seeking, or having gained, the award.

In 1995 the government started 'Modern Apprenticeships' grants, for vocational training of 16 and 17 year olds. The new (from 1997) Labour government was also considering more training initiatives to encourage businesses in that area of risk.

Types of training

Consider some specific examples, e.g. related to a case firm.

- On-the-job – while at work, delivered by in-house training personnel or by bought-in specialists.
- Off-the-job – carried out at a location other than the workplace.
- Part-time – includes day-release, evening classes and short courses, which may or may not be during normal working hours.
- Full-time – either short- or long-term courses, perhaps in more complex aspects of the work, out of the workplace for an extended period.

Reasons for training

- Technological changes to product, process or working methods [see Topic 7 Operations management, p. 83 Work study] e.g. CIM lathes, or new office-computer software.
- Health and Safety, e.g. for using computers, or handling industrial materials, within new legislation [see p. 51 The Law: EU Health and Safety Directives 1992].
- Improvement in performance to reduce costs and/or improve quality, to remain competitive [see Topic 7 Operations management, p. 76 Costs and p. 87 Quality (including *kaizen*)].
- Job changes may require re-training, e.g. a spot-welder in car production requiring redeployment after robot-welding machines introduced.
- Rewards/perks – e.g. an all-expenses-paid training course at some pleasant venue, although also improving the individuals' performance within the business!

Why businesses hesitate

C.E.P!

- Costs of some types of training can be high (particularly if not 'in-house') e.g. £3 m. to train RAF Harrier pilots...4/98: first pilot to take legally-entitled maternity leave.
- Effects of the training (even with effective appraisal methods) may be difficult and/or expensive to quantify precisely, e.g. a teacher attending an INSET course!
- Poaching of trained workers by other businesses may be a problem, e.g. in the highly competitive computer software markets.

Many businesses apparently use 'Training Needs Analysis' (TNA), as a method of exposing areas which would benefit from training. It involves the answers to three questions:
- What are the organisation's short- and medium-term goals?
- What range of tasks and how much of each will be needed?
- To what extent are they present in the current workforce?

The fastest growing industry in the world, too!

> 'Britain's tourist industry risks losing out to other European competitors unless it resolves problems of poor pay and training, according to a report [by the accountants Coopers and Lybrand and the London Business School] for the National Heritage Department...It said: "In an increasingly competitive international market we cannot afford to ignore consumer research that suggests that the quality and value for money of our tourist product does not always meet the customer's expectation." The report goes on to state that 45% of full-time staff and 74% of part-timers had received no job-related training. The figures gave "cause for concern" as 55% of all staff are part-time.'
>
> The Times (31/10/96).

Any aspect you would include, or leave out?

Training often begins with new employees being given an induction course, e.g. for a bank...

TRAINING DEPARTMENT INDUCTION COURSE

Date __ / __ / __

PROGRAMME

- role of UK banks in society
- the Mission Statement, business objectives, and your role in helping to meet them
- the Bank's main products
- the Bank's customer service
- communication and teamwork
- telephone techniques
- personal development opportunities

Designing a training programme

H. T. Graham and R. Bennett, in *Human Resources Management* (1992), outlined the procedures:

A P P R O A C H
- **A**nalyse job
- **P**erformance standards – to be aimed at
- **P**erformance attained – already being achieved
- **R**equirements of training
- **O**riginate training programme
- **A**dminister training
- **C**heck results – goals achieved?
- **H**ow can training be improved next time?

> 'The BBC is spending millions of pounds a year on management and business courses for its staff, including day-long seminars for its 150 most senior executives...The first lecture last week was by American management guru Tom Peters, whose 7-hour talk was said by one executive to be full of "aphorisms like Forrest Gump's 'Life is like a box of chocolates'". The BBC refused to reveal how much it cost, but Tom Peters' company says it was "well over £10,000"...
>
> All BBC departments are currently finalising lengthy reports for the annual review, in which they are judged on whether they have delivered promises of performance.'
>
> The Observer (9/4/95).

Change

A crucial aspect of Business, so increasingly likely in exam questions.

A main theme of Tom Peters' conferences and seminars to business people is that businesses and their employees must be ready to change quickly, even be ready to reinvent themselves.

> 'Crazy times call for crazy organisations. Crazy companies need crazy people!'
>
> Tom Peters (1994).

Change is inevitable – the problem is how to get people in an organisation to accept it, and then use it to the best advantage [see Topic 4 Management and leadership].

> 'It is becoming widely recognised that the structure of employment is changing for good and the days of a job for life are over. The key to future success is training: everyone must broaden and constantly update their skills and learn to thrive on change rather than fear it. Organisations with well trained employees will reap benefits and enhancing the skills of existing staff is the most cost-effective way forward.'
>
> The Industrial Society's *Briefing Plus* (September 1995).

Reasons for resistance

Relate to a particular example, e.g. in an exam case study.

- Feelings of insecurity generated by intended change.
- Disruption of existing relations, e.g. in groups/teams.
- Threats to status and/or pay (and perks?).
- Influence of the culture and group norms, perhaps opposing the change.
- Doubts over feasibility of proposed changes.
- Concern over having to retrain and acquire new skills.
- Fear of new technology, e.g. new computer system and/or software.
- Resentment over not being consulted.

Has there been a change in your life recently? How do you view it?

> *'Do you resist change, or embrace it? For some, even one change is too many. For others, change means progress...'*
>
> Advertisement for Lexus cars (4/98).

Overcoming resistance

Industrial psychologist Kurt Lewin suggests three steps:

- **unfreezing** – disposing of existing practices and ideas in the way of change
- **changing** – teaching employees to think and perform differently
- **refreezing** – establishing new norms and standard practice.

How did you find the change from GCSE work to A level work?

Use external consultants?

Many larger businesses employ external consultants to advise on and manage required changes.

Advantages:
- more objective
- experience from other similar organisations and problems
- no vested interests in the welfare of particular departments
- not involved in internal politics
- up-to-date knowledge of relevant specialist techniques.

Evaluation! Similar factors to 'internal or external recruitment'.

Disadvantages:
- not as familiar with the organisation, its methods, and where to get information
- not so accountable for their actions, with future career not so directly connected
- can be expensive.

Types of change affecting the human resources

Find examples of each type in newspapers.

(a) Restructuring or downsizing

Such major change will significantly affect a workforce. In order to increase efficiency and cut costs, there may be cutbacks in the labour force, through natural wastage and/or redundancies.

Terms understood?

> *'NatWest was criticised by unions after it confirmed that it would cut "at least" 10,000 more jobs and close 200 branches by the year 2000. B.I.F.U., the banking union, said NatWest's decision would hit some communities very hard and called for a rethink...'*
>
> The Times (5/12/96).

(b) Introducing new technology

Its introduction would require:
- precise definition of the operational changes needed
- how new working methods will affect particular individuals and groups
- identifying the current attitudes and related working practices
- stating attitudes necessary for people to adapt successfully to the change
- measures to be put in to change existing attitudes, including retraining.

Unwelcome change

Way back!

There were no unions to negotiate on the introduction of new technology.

Luddites were gangs of impoverished stocking and lace makers in Nottingham, who, from 1811, vandalised new mills and machines that threatened their livelihoods. Production had changed from the traditional skilled cottage industry, to factories where the weavers objected to poor conditions, long hours, meagre wages and the inferior-quality hosiery. According to legend, the first machine breaking happened by accident – a 'feeble-minded lad' called Ned Ludd was responsible! During winter 1811–12, Luddites smashed 'frames' almost every night. It spread to Lancashire and Yorkshire, although participants were risking transportation or even execution. A mass trial in York in 1813 led to 17 executions for 'machine-breaking and murder'. The movement finished in 1816 after a Loughborough mill had been wrecked, and seven Luddites executed.

Welcome change

Not that far back!

In 1976, at the Volvo factory, at Kalmar in Sweden, it was decided to change the traditional **division of labour** production. There were high rates of absenteeism and labour turnover, mainly from the boring and repetitive work.

For the new large up-market 760 saloons and estates, teams of (15–20) car workers were made responsible for completing a complete section of the car, e.g. the steering system, or electrics. They decided between them how tasks were allocated and when breaks could be taken. A large investment capital was needed, to make alterations to the factory and the technology involved. The results of the changes were lower productivity but, crucially, better quality. Levels of workers' job satisfaction and motivation had risen [see Topic 7 Operations management, p. 88 Quality circles].

(c) Merger or takeover

> 'Half of all takeovers fail. The main reason they fail is that they do not carry the people with them...A take-over is a great time for change and staff are only too happy to change if they are approached correctly.'
>
> Professor John Hunt, The London Business School.

More recent!

Between 1989 and 1994, the Woolwich Building Society took over four other building societies, a chain of estate agents and a banking subsidiary. The most recent acquisition was the Town and Country Building Society – judged to be the fastest growing society in 1992.

What were the main business objectives?

> 'In the past when we took over a society, we could afford to let the growth in the market soak up any excess capacity and duplication. Now, we have to be ruthless. The Town and Country, when we took them over, employed 750, but by the end of the year only 200 will remain...We have always told the staff association at the old Town and Country what our intentions were; there has been no phoney bill of goods. We have consulted at every level and have honoured all the very generous redundancy agreements...Of course you feel sorry for those that felt they had a guaranteed career in a dynamic organisation, but I must put the health of the Woolwich as my first priority.'
>
> D. Kirkham, Chief Executive of the Woolwich, The Times, (12/6/94).

Professor John Hunt, after research into several takeovers and the effects on workers, devised a **six-point plan** for minimising human casualties:

- Explain the rationale and benefits of the takeover, and give timetable of integration between the organisations.

- Integrate policies quickly.

- Clarify terms and conditions of employment [see Relocation below].

- Check the policy on redundancy, and choose the most generous possible (although involving extra costs).

- Identify key personnel, and 'stroke those who must stay'.

- Label managers: 'High potential, Short-term essential, Potential elsewhere in the organisation, *or* No potential'.

(d) Relocation

In 1995, 27% of small and larger businesses in the UK were considering relocation by the year 2000, mainly to reduce indirect costs/overheads [see Topic 7 Operations management, p. 73 Location], according to a survey by 'Black Horse Relocation'. An increasing number of new employee contracts apparently include...'agreeing to a relocation anywhere within the UK' or 'within a 25-mile radius of...', but a relocation could cause problems for some employees.

E.g.:

- In February 1995 the courts found in favour of an employee who refused to relocate from Scarborough to Hull (in Yorkshire), because of a 40-mile journey each way on bad roads each day. He received a redundancy package from his former employers, but the solicitors did warn that, 'If there is a proper relocation clause in your contract, you will usually have to abide by it if you want to keep your job.'

- Many women provide second incomes for their families, and may find it difficult to move. Relocation clauses might thus form a bar to their promotion prospects, so the Court of Appeal has ruled (in 1995) that such clauses can constitute sexual discrimination.

However an employment lawyer at a leading firm of London solicitors concluded (in 1995) that, 'Most employers will be able to get away with it by saying it is objectively justified.'

> 'The requirement for a more mobile workforce is going to make life difficult for people who expected to settle down in one place when they come to bring up a family. On the other hand, managers are now so highly skilled that they are difficult to replace.'
>
> The Observer (24/9/95).

Harvard Business School graduate Ricardo Semler made major changes to the family firm Semco Engineering, in São Paulo, Brazil. It has become a famous example of industrial democracy [see Topic 4 Management and leadership, p.15 Leadership]. When senior managers decided expansion was possible only at a new location, they arranged for workers to travel by coaches to three possible sites, and to choose the new site by ballot. Their choice was accepted, although it was not the managers' favourite because it was close to a business which had experienced recent industrial relations problems.

> 'A turtle may live for hundreds of years because it is well protected by its shell, but only moves forward when it sticks its head out!'
>
> Ricardo Semler of Semco Engineering, at NHS managers' conference (1995).

> 'The most important stakeholder in the company is not the shareholder, not even the customer, but it is the staff.'
>
> Richard Branson, Chairman of Virgin Management Ltd (1994).

> 'I believe increasingly that in the future the organisation will have to adapt to the needs of the individual, rather than expecting the individual to adapt to the needs of the organisation.'
>
> Sir John Harvey-Jones, Making It Happen (1988).

Communication

The transmission of a message and its receipt

A successful organisation needs to have effective communication – internally and with external stakeholders. It will include data, opinions/views and sentiments/feelings/emotions, with 'noise' – any form of interference that produces distracting information. There are four types of communication:

- **verbal** – face-to-face, or by telephone, presentation, or discussion
- **non-verbal** – by gesture, posture, eye contact, tone of voice, physical appearance and presentation
- **written** – by letter, E-mail, fax, memo, report, visual aids, noticeboards etc.
- **numerical** – by tables of data, bar charts, histograms, pie charts and graphs.

Symptoms of poor communication

- low morale
- higher labour turnover
- unwillingness to make decisions and/or accept responsibility
- conflict and/or aggression

- absenteeism
- more production errors or higher 'scrap rate'
- evidence of lack of control and discipline.

Skills:

- listening
- speaking
- reading
- writing
- using IT

> 'Government and business are trying to prepare the existing and future workforce for the rapidly changing demands of employers by promoting the concept of "lifetime learning"...Little attention has been given in the past to how non-managerial workers should be equipped with the skills to embrace change [see p. 34 Change] and to communicate their needs effectively.'
>
> The Guardian (7/10/95).

Barriers to effective communication

(a) Organisational:

- inadequate machinery for communication e.g. lack of upward vertical channels for feedback
- 'Chinese Whispers' message distortion

- information overload
- status, e.g. differences in seniority
- inappropriate method/medium chosen

(b) Semantics: [i.e. use of words]

- technical jargon
- words the receiver is not used to

- ambiguities

Which apply to the case under consideration.

The first one is often the main problem, e.g. for management not gaining feedback.

O.S.H.!

Consider some examples, e.g. in an exam case study.

(c) Human feelings:

- individual bias
- stereotyping [see below]
- distraction
- issues of change
- emotions
- inappropriate body language
- deliberate manipulation.

Both of these are apparently very common in the business world. What problems can result?

The halo effect – the assumption that, because an individual exhibits **one** characteristic, they necessarily possess other characteristics as well, e.g. if a presentable candidate for a job is assumed to be intelligent and industrious as well.

Stereotyping – another type of labelling, where an individual is immediately put, mentally, in a particular category of people and assumed to possess all the characteristics of that group.

> 'Managers can handle stress if they fully understand why it is happening. If they are part of the strategic decision-making, then they will accept increased workload. In the end it's all about communication. 88% of managers we surveyed found poor internal communications to be a source of stress.'
>
> Managers under Stress report by The Institute of Management (1994).

Improving communication

Perfect communication is an impossible objective, but an organisation will benefit from relative improvements.

> 'The company must ensure there are good lines of communication all the way from the front line to top management and back again.'
>
> David Clutterbuck in The Power of Empowerment (1994).

Improvements can be made by:

- ensuring employees are aware of communication problems
- using more than one communication net/system
- minimising communication chain linkages
- reducing status differentials, e.g. open-plan offices or all employees using the same cafeteria
- careful composition of messages, encouraging simplicity and clarity
- using different media to reinforce the message
- encouraging recognition of cultural and social differences, prejudices and interdepartmental rivalries
- using and encouraging upward communication channels, e.g. appraisals [see p. 31 Appraisals], staff meetings, suggestion boxes, procedures for solving grievances, for feedback.

Another useful list for an exam answer.

> 'A massive change is taking place in employee communications – once the Cinderella of the communications world. The galloping pace of global competition and technological development is forcing companies to respond faster to what's happening in the marketplace. If employees are to be empowered to act, they need to be better informed then ever before.
>
> The mission of employee communications is to help make employees – and therefore the whole organisation – more effective in achieving individual, team and organisational objectives [see Topic 2 Objectives]. However, communication is not just about sending information. It's a two-way process that involves listening, so we are hoping for a lot of feedback...'
>
> IBM's in-house newspaper, Read Me (9/96).

Chris Roebuck of the City University Business School also emphasises the importance of feedback, and recommends that managers should:

- acknowledge employees as experts who know about their jobs
- encourage employee contributions at any time, not just in briefings or surveys
- take immediate action when points are raised
- set a time limit to respond on more complex issues. Say what is happening, and if action is taken as a result of feedback, always say so because this tells employees that the organisation is both listening and acting.

Listen!

'A lot of communication in organisations is downward, from managers to employees. **Feedback** *is the other half of the communication equation. Senior managers think they know what's going on further down, but they need feedback to understand what is really happening.*

The problem with the traditional method of gathering information is that it focuses on **hard feedback***, i.e. production figures, accounts and other statistical data, which provides only part of the picture.* **Soft feedback***, i.e. employees' views, perceptions and ideas are often neglected, creating a culture that at best makes employees feel their views are not valued and at worst means they are frightened to speak up, even when they know something is going wrong.'*

Chris Roebuck, in *Effective Feedback: Recipe for Success* (1995).

'Ask the man doing the job.'

Dr W. E. Deming [see p. 22 Motivation].

Not p.c., but when was Dr Deming giving this advice? [see p. 26].

Using Information Technology

Information processing:
- word processing
- database
- spreadsheets
- Computer Aided Design (CAD).

Information transmission:
- computer networks
- mobile telecommunications
- e-mail
- faxes
- Electronic Funds Transfer (EFT)
- teleconferencing.

[See Topic 8 Data and information technology].

Communicating externally

Consider the case of a well-known plc.

A business will communicate with the public via:
- marketing mix – including **p**roduct, **p**rice, **p**romotion, **p**lace [see Topic 6 Marketing]
- Annual Report and Accounts – expert comments?
- treatment of its workforce, e.g. redundancies
- treatment of its customers, e.g. complaints.

A 1995 survey of large European companies showed that nearly 80% of them offered language training to staff as a matter of course, and English features in the schools' curriculum of most European countries. Another (1995) survey, of UK businesses, found that as many as 74% of foreign language calls were abandoned at the switchboard!

Do you need a translation?

'If I'm selling to you, I speak your language. If I'm buying from you...dann müssen Sie Deutsch sprechen.'

Herr Willy Brandt, Chancellor of (West) Germany, in 1985.

The Single Market

- Began officially on 1st January 1993.
- Consists of all the EU countries – 15 since 1995.
- An attempt to eliminate, or at least reduce, barriers to trade.
- Main advantage for UK businesses: **more consumers** than the USA and Japan combined.
- Main disadvantage for UK businesses: **more competition**, e.g. from French insurance companies.

Increasingly important – evidenced by the countries expressing a desire to join in the future. It is a huge market.

'British companies can only benefit from recruiting staff [see p. 29 Recruitment] who have a knowledge of the language and culture of countries which are trading partners.'

The Guardian (7/10/95).

'No matter how articulate people are, if the organisation is a bad communicator it can be difficult for the individual to develop.'

Christine Wright, communications consultant, The Industrial Society (1993).

Link with Maslow's 'Hierarchy of Needs'.

Trade Unions

'A continuous association of wage earners for the purpose of maintaining or improving the conditions of their working lives.'

S. and B. Webb, The History of Trade Unionism.

Industrial relations is communication between representatives of employers and the representatives of employees. In 1995 approximately nine million UK workers – 30% of the country's workforce, belonged to unions. (It was about 50% in the 1970s and early '80s.) Many other workers will be affected by the actions of unions, e.g. negotiations for pay on a national scale.

The main objectives.

'We are here to protect people. The union movement is about individuals, about the right of a man to have a decent living standard and to stand up and answer the boss back.'

Len Murray, ex-General Secretary of the Trades Union Congress (TUC).

Collective bargaining is where workers in particular factories, businesses or even whole industries have pay negotiated by a union – 'Unity is Strength' from the union's point of view. A union might be involved in negotiating on:

- basic rates of pay – time- or piece-rate
- bonuses – for overtime, unsocial hours or productivity
- working conditions/environment – ergonomics? [see Topic 7 Operations management, p. 84 The working environment]
- work schedules and production targets – attainable? [see Topic 2 Objectives, p. 8 Management by objectives]
- grievances – 'a cause for complaint'
- disputes – 'a disagreement with the management'
- hours – a shorter working week max. 48 hrs
- Health and Safety at Work [see p. 49 The Law].

Types of unions

- **Craft** – the original unions, based on the skills of a particular trade/occupation, e.g. (steam) train drivers and firemen.

- **Industrial** – for all workers in an industry, giving greater bargaining power but perhaps simpler negotiations for management. Most UK examples have split up, e.g. National Union of Democratic Mineworkers (NUDM) separated from the NUM.

- **General** – some of Britain's largest, e.g. UNISON (for public sector workers, and the largest) and the Transport and General Workers Union (TGWU), with greater finance and more 'industrial muscle'. However, disputes can arise between members, e.g. lorry drivers greeting the 1970s container [transport] revolution, but dockworkers striking in protest. The 1990s saw mergers, to achieve greater economies of scale.

- **White-collar** – for non-manual workers, e.g. teachers, office workers, bank staff. ('Blue-collar' refers to skilled manual workers, whose overalls were originally blue.) Membership of this type grew in the 1980s, against the overall trend [see below].

A typical union organisational chart:

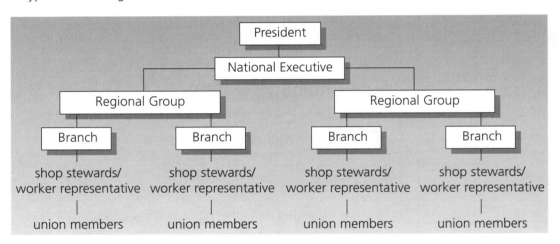

The **Trades Union Congress (TUC)** is itself a union, of most of the larger unions. It represents their views, e.g. on economic events, in a similar way to that in which the **Confederation of British Industries (CBI)** speaks for its large-business members. The May 1995 White Paper 'Fairness at Work' said that unions will not have to be recognised unless 40% of (eligible) workers vote in favour, but the TUC says recognition will benefit the business itself.

- Unions make it more difficult for an employer to 'hire and fire', so workforce planning will be improved over the longer term [see p. 30 Human resource planning].

- Unions encourage the training and personal development of their members, so achieving a higher investment in skills and ensuring a better return on capital [see Topic 9 Finance, p. 104 ROCE].

- Unions are positive in the way that they press for change, recognising the need for companies to remain competitive in their markets.

Key aspects in the development of unions

- The origins of the first trade unions were in providing some basic protection, e.g. for a worker losing a job because of a day's illness, in the factory system resulting from The Industrial Revolution (after the 1770s).

- Early attempts to form unions (e.g. in the 1840s) failed partly because of strong political resistance, from worries about a possible French Revolution (1789)-style uprising in Britain, and also most workers were poorly educated and therefore difficult to communicate with and organise. They also had little income to spare on a union subscription. Unions could not raise finance to get better organised until those for skilled manual workers.

- Determinants of strength/bargaining power include an important good or service, raising sufficient finance (based on average pay of members), willingness to take industrial action, e.g. a strike, and apparently sex – a predominantly male union is historically more willing to flex the industrial muscle.

- 'The British Disease', was the number of working days lost due to strikes (i.e. number of days x number of workers), particularly during the 1970s. Some (Tory) newspapers had headlines such as *'Holding the nation to ransom!'* and *'Who rules the country?'*, and there was political debate about the influence of the unions.

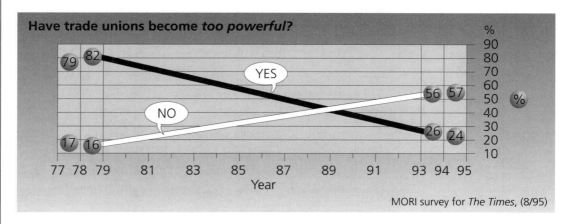

Have trade unions become *too powerful?*

MORI survey for *The Times*, (8/95)

The number of working days lost through strikes was relatively low in the 1990s, especially compared to 'The Winter of Discontent' 1978–79 – resulting from unions' frustration with the Labour government's attempts to extend pay (increased restriction) policies [see Topic 10 External influences, p. 121] …Margaret Thatcher (Conservative) would become Britain's first woman PM in the 1979 election. February 1984 to February 1985 saw a miners' strike, over disputed closures of 'uneconomic pits', which significantly raised the average number of working days lost.

Why 'single union'?

Keep checking in newspapers for recent developments.

What reasons would you be prepared to go on strike for? What would you not strike for?

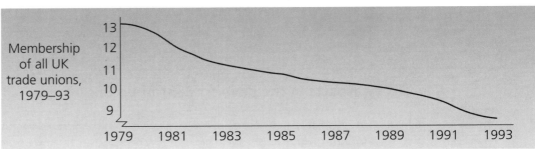

Working days lost 1979–94 (millions)

29.5 12.0   27.1

8
6
4
2
0

79 80 81 82 83 84 85 86 87 88 89 90 91 92 93 94
Year

Department of Employment: Financial Times (7/95)

Membership of all UK trade unions, 1979–93

13
12
11
10
9

1979   1981   1983   1985   1987   1989   1991   1993

CSO Annual Abstract, Employment Gazette (6/94)

Reasons for the decline in membership:

- Younger workers relating unions to traditional industries and 'the working class', rather than the services jobs in the 1990s, and the image of some unions as bureaucratic and inefficient, and perhaps not worth an annual subscription.

- Recession and resultant unemployment [see Topic 10 External influences] meant many workers no longer qualified for membership or could afford it.

- Large numbers of redundancies in UK manufacturing (– the usual measure of 'deindustrialisation') confirmed to some workers how ineffective unions had become.

- Japanese and other multinationals investing in plants in Britain, particularly welcomed during the 1980s because of the job creation, led the trend towards single-union, or even no-union, agreements.

- The expense of industrial action made strikes in particular less attractive, perhaps making membership of a union less important.

- Reduced income, from the declining membership, in turn prevented more expensive marketing to enhance attractiveness – a vicious circle.

- Conservative government policy 1980–93 – partly to reduce union influence, e.g.:
  - *Employment Act 1980:* a new code of practice said there must be a maximum of six **pickets** outside a workplace, with no threatening (or violent) behaviour allowed.
  - *Employment Act 1982:* a **closed shop** allowed only if 80% of workers vote in favour (with 85% needing to be in favour of continuing one).
  - There were other *Employment Acts* in 1988, 1989 and 1990.
  - *Trade Union Act 1990:* a **strike** only became official, i.e. backed by the union, if a majority voted in favour (in a secret ballot).
  - *Trade Union and Labour Relations (Consolidation) Act 1992:* included that employers could not collect union dues/subscriptions without written consent from individual workers.

'Allowing managers to manage' (Lady Thatcher)

or

'Union-bashing' (Labour/Opposition party)

Why?

Again, change.

A new marketing strategy was needed, to improve the image.

Which would be the most damaging to the production of a business?

Can you see both sides (even if you disagree with one of them)?

'Trade unions have to operate in a hostile and rapidly changing environment [see Topic 10 External influences]. They have shown a readiness to adapt to imposed change in a number of ways. They appear to be developing a more professional approach to the changing labour market and the arrival of new management thinking... Some have begun to launch recruitment campaigns among women, ethnic minorities and part-time workers.'

Robert Taylor, *The Future of Trade Unions* (1994).

In 1998 the total membership figure was still around 9 million workers, but it was rising. UNISON, the biggest UK union, led the marketing campaigns to increase membership, with national press and television advertising.

Forms of industrial action

Individuals or groups may take unorganised action in terms of absenteeism, high labour turnover, apathy, poor performance, complaints etc. Trade unions can take a number of forms of organised industrial action.

- **Strike** – the ultimate industrial weapon, involving members withdrawing their labour. Production will cease and the employer will lose revenue. An 'unofficial strike' is one not officially approved by the union, often creating extra problems.

- **Picketing** – when representatives of a union stand outside the place of work, to persuade (peacefully) workers to join the strike and not cross the picket line. Those who do may be labelled 'scabs'. 'Secondary picketing', where workers from one place of work picket another, to bolster strike action, is illegal.

- **Withdrawal of goodwill** – where workers are obstructive on aspects of work that have previously required co-operation.

- **Go-slow** – where workers perform the usual tasks but deliberately take longer.

- **Work-to-rule** – where workers stick precisely to the exact contract, job description or rule book, in order to reduce overall efficiency, e.g. if railway workers were to check every carriage door before a train departs.

- **Ban on overtime** – where workers will only work the minimum number of hours stated in the contract. Some businesses have come to rely on overtime.

- **Sit-in** – where some workers occupy their place of work, perhaps overnight, for publicity purposes and/or to prevent production.

- **Blacking** – where workers refuse to use raw materials or machinery, e.g. if their union reports that imports are causing redundancies of fellow (UK?) workers. Workers, e.g. who did not join a strike, could also be 'blacked'.

Solving disputes

Example: In July 1995 ASLEF, the union representing most British Rail train drivers, announced a ballot result in favour of a series of one-day strikes. The 'final' offer from management had been a 3% increase in basic pay – judged too low and too late by the union.

'ASLEF is anxious for an improved settlement because this will be the last central pay deal before privatisation, after which negotiations will be conducted with 40 different companies, so reducing the union's industrial muscle...

ASLEF members have voted for industrial action at a time of increasing unhappiness about their working conditions and the industry's future. They claim they are over-worked because there are 1,200 fewer drivers than a year ago for the same number of trains; and they say safety is at risk because they work an average of nine hours longer than the maximum 39-hour week.'

The Observer (9/7/95).

> *'Most people and businesses will not be affected by the ASLEF strikes. In big commuting areas, such as London and the South-East, and for business travel between cities, train usage is much higher...On a normal day, about 720,000 people travel to London by train or by London Underground, while only about 150,000 come in by car.*
>
> *BR is claiming losses of £10 million for each strike day...Strikes, of course, are costly for those taking part in them. BR calculates that ASLEF's members will each lose about £400 if they take part in all 6 strikes.'*
>
> The Times (14/7/95).

After two one-day strikes (with London Underground drivers joining the second one) agreement with the management was reached – a 3.3% basic pay increase plus, in 1996, a reduction in working hours. Both sides of the dispute claimed victory!

Disputes can also involve a smaller group of workers or an individual.

Know how these terms differ from each other.

Some important terms:

- **Resignation** – where the individual worker voluntarily decides to end his or her employment with that organisation, possibly under pressure to do so, or simply to go to a more attractive alternative.

- **Retirement** – where the employee comes to the end of the contracted period. It is usually based on number of years served and/or age, but an increasing number of individuals take early retirement. A company, Civil Service, Armed Services, or other pension, might be applicable.

- **Redeployment** – where an employee relocates to another job and/or department, perhaps in preference to either of the following alternatives.

- **Redundancy –** where the job being performed by the employee is no longer required. Simply finding a better replacement worker would not be legal [see p. 48 The Law: Employment Protection (Consolidation) Act 1978].

- **Dismissal** – where the worker is informed that they will no longer be employed by the organisation. To be fair, legally, it can be for:

  - either inability to perform the work required in spite of suitable training provided by the employer, and several provable (e.g. three) warnings about the unsatisfactory standard of work.

  - or misconduct e.g. persistent lateness or minor infractions of discipline, after several informal warnings (best if logged), then a formal oral warning by a manager in the presence of the supervisor and a union representative, and finally a formal written warning.

  - **Summary dismissal**, i.e. instant, without the warnings, is legal in the case of serious/gross misconduct, e.g. if drunkenness had endangered people's lives.

  - **Unfair dismissal** would be 'for no justifiable reason'. It can only be claimed (as with redundancy payments) after an individual has worked for an employer for **over one year** (Reduced from 'two years' employment', after the May 1998 White Paper 'Fairness at Work'.) However, if an employee is dismissed because of membership (or non-membership) of a union, or refusal to work for health and safety reasons, or taking legal proceedings because of (provable) sexual, racial or disability discrimination, then an Industrial Tribunal would rule 'unfair dismissal' even if the length of employment is under a year.

Both managers and employees benefit from a clear set of workable **negotiating procedures**, perhaps with union assistance, to resolve collective or individual disputes within the organisation. The procedures normally include:

- First: *first-line* managers may be able to resolve individual disputes directly and quickly. ACAS [see over] recommends individuals should be allowed to be supported by a recognised union official or fellow employee.

Could you apply this to an example dispute, e.g. in a case study? Can you understand both sides' views?

- Second: if a dispute remains unresolved, ACAS recommends that the next stage should be an appeal heard by a manager at a higher level or from a different area of the organisation.

- Third: where a dispute *still* remains unresolved, the next stage may have to involve a third party, not necessarily the law courts (where cases may be lengthy and expensive), but perhaps the matter could be settled by ACAS.

Advisory, Conciliation and Arbitration Service

'The mission of ACAS is to improve the performance and effectiveness of organisations by providing an independent and impartial service to prevent and resolve disputes and to build harmonious relationships at work.'

ACAS was set up by the government in 1974, particularly because of the number of working days lost to disputes in the workplace, and is an independent organisation managed by a council of nine members – three chosen by the TUC, three by the CBI, and three who are independent.

'Issues in procedure should be resolved as close to their point of origin as possible.'

If there is deadlock in a dispute the parties may ask ACAS to help:

Arbitration – when the parties put their case, usually first in writing and then orally at a subsequent hearing, to an independent arbitrator, appointed from the ACAS panel of experienced individuals. The parties will have agreed in advance that the arbitrator's decision is binding as a means of finally resolving the dispute.

Mediation – where, instead of a binding decision, the ACAS mediator provides one or more formal recommendations for the parties to consider as a means of resolving the dispute.

You'll need to understand the differences between these three.

Conciliation – where attempts are made to resolve a dispute by ACAS arranging informal discussions, perhaps first with each of the parties separately, and then with both parties together.

ACAS also undertakes research into all aspects of industrial relations, publishes statistics, and publishes booklets and reports to encourage good practice.

Of all the cases concerning individual disputes, only about a third remain unresolved and move on to a further stage.

Industrial tribunals

Renamed **Employment tribunals**, they have been part of the UK legal system since 1964, with members expert in legislation on workplace disputes.

The old name still seems to be used more often.

- The main task of industrial tribunals is settling **unfair dismissal** complaints – the 25% not resolved by ACAS.

- Each tribunal has an experienced lawyer as chairperson, plus two lay people – one nominated by the CBI, the other by the TUC.

- Approximately one-third of unfair dismissal complaints are upheld, but although firms may seem to have won, the costs to them in terms of time, expense, and possibly bad publicity may outweigh victory benefits.

- Individuals found to have been unfairly dismissed can claim compensation (for loss of earnings and pension), with the previous maximum of £12,000 to be removed by law in 1998, and re-instatement or re-engagement (not necessarily wanted?)

- Appeals can be made on a point of law to the **Employment Appeals Tribunal (EAT)**, consisting of a High Court judge and two lay persons. In rare cases an appeal may be allowed to an Appeals Court.

- A complaint reaching an industrial tribunal usually means the particular business needs to review its industrial relations practices, in order to prevent further such damaging cases arising.

The Law

The two functions of the Law.

Laws can **constrain** businesses, e.g. on Health and Safety [see below] or they can **encourage** them [e.g. see Topic 1 Types of businesses, p. 5 Limited liability, or Topic 7 Operations management, p. 75 Intellectual property].

The UK has been a full member of The European Union (since 1973), and signed the Maastricht Treaty (in 1991), so agreeing to closer ties in the future. Community Law applies in the UK:

- **Regulations** (e.g. in 1981) apply directly to the EU's population and automatically form part of the Law in member states, giving individual rights and duties which national courts must recognise.

- **Directives** (e.g. in 1988 and 1993) are binding on the (15) member states but not directly applicable, i.e. the UK has a certain amount of time in which to decide how to implement the directive.

- **Decisions** are directly binding but they are addressed to specific individuals or organisations within the member states, and not to the population generally.

A body of UK and EU labour law has been built up to protect the interests of people when in the workplace, e.g.:

(a) Contracts

A key piece of law.

Employment Protection (Consolidation) Act 1978

Stated that a contract has to be handed to employees within 13 weeks of employment starting, and that it must include:

What does 'consolidation' mean in this case?

- the job title
- the parties involved (i.e. employer and employee)
- the date when employment began
- the rate of pay, how calculated and when paid
- rules regarding working hours
- entitlement to holidays
- rules on sickness and injury
- details of any pension scheme
- minimum length of notice required by both parties to end employment
- disciplinary rules affecting employees (unless business employs <20)
- name of person to whom a grievance can be taken.

Trade Union Reform and Employment Rights Act 1993

This added that, if a worker is employed for more than one month, they must be supplied with a statement of the main terms of the contract within two months of starting. Any changes must be notified a month in advance. Even if an employer fails to provide the legal requirements, an employee still has some basic legal rights, e.g. against unfair dismissal.

Employers' Liability (Compulsory Insurance) Act 1969

Insisted on insurance of employees against injury and disease resulting from their employment. Employers have to display a valid Certificate of Insurance in the place of work.

(b) Health and safety

After the Industrial Revolution the main emphasis was on mass production, to achieve economies of scale for ensuring competitiveness in rapidly increasing markets, in the UK and abroad. The early 1900s saw some basic legislation on the workplace, but injuries, e.g. losing fingers in cutlery production, were seen as occupational hazards – no compensation unless, unusually, an individual had arranged insurance. Agriculture, construction and mining remained particularly dangerous. Trade unions often negotiated with a firm or industry, on matters affecting their members, and helped to formulate new legislation, via contacts with the Labour Party and the influence of the TUC. The main period of union growth coincided with legislation which formed the base of current health and safety provision.

Factories Act 1961

Consolidated previous Acts, in three main areas:

- Health – e.g. regular cleaning of work areas, a minimum space of 400 cubic feet per worker, a minimum temperature of 60 °F for sedentary workers, adequate lighting and ventilation, adequate toilet facilities, and alternative accommodation where toxic fumes may be present.
- Safety – e.g. dangerous parts of machinery to be fenced off, lifting equipment to be well made and maintained, and fire precautions to include compulsory fire certification for every factory, exits being kept clear and unlocked, and (where more than 20 employees) an established fire drill which is known to all.
- Welfare – e.g. drinking water, adequate washing and cloakroom facilities, seating for workers (where it would not interfere with the type of work) and adequate first aid facilities – all injuries to be recorded.

Offices, Shops and Railway Premises Act 1963

Covered physical working conditions, but not just in factories. Provisions covered the minimum space (of 12 square metres) per person, and adequate cleanliness, lighting, heating, fresh air/ventilation, washing and sanitary facilities, drinking water, first aid, fire precautions, unacceptable noise levels, lifting of heavy weights, and notification of accidents.

Employers' Liability (Compulsory Insurance) Act 1969

Made compulsory the insurance of all employees against injury and disease resulting from their employment, with employers having to display valid certificates in the place of work.

Employment Medical Advisory Act 1972

Set up the Employment Medical Advisory Service to advise employers, employees and trade unions on 'occupational medicine', including effects of jobs on health, medical standards, minimising health hazards, and problems faced by disabled employees.

Health and Safety at Work Act 1974

Supplemented the existing legislation, to ensure provision of safe working conditions free from health hazards, for example to cover the 5 million self-employed workers not previously protected. The HSWA established a responsibility of the employer *and* employees to provide a safe workplace.

Can you apply relevant legislation to a case study organisation?

HSW

A crucial piece of law.

Not just employers.

Duties of employers

- Providing workplaces and methods of work that are safe, and ensuring that machines are well maintained.
- Ensuring that machines and chemicals are used, stored and transported safely.
- Providing sufficient information, training and supervision to ensure health and safety.
- Maintaining safe premises with safe exits, entrances and working environment – with adequate heating, lighting, ventilation, toilets etc.
- Providing a written safety policy (where five+ workers) and communicating it.
- Recording and reporting all accidents, especially if a worker has three+ days off.

Duties of employees

- Taking reasonable care to avoid injury to self or workmates.
- Following the health and safety regulations that apply there.
- Co-operating with the employer to ensure a safe workplace.
- Behaving in a sensible manner at all times, and not misusing equipment.

If an accident occurs because a worker did not follow correct safety procedures, e.g. not wearing the protective clothing provided, the employee may be prosecuted as well as the employer.

Health and Safety Executive (HSE)

This body includes representatives of employers, employees and local authorities, and was formed to back up the HSWA. HSE's inspectors check the law is being observed. Regulations may vary according to particular industries, e.g. for offshore oil and gas platforms. Inspectors can enter any workplace for inspection or investigation.

Prohibition notice: forbids any activity that could lead to injury until the problem is rectified (and inspected again).

Improvement notice: gives an employer a set amount of time to rectify a safety problem. Inspectors can prosecute employers for non-observance or negligence (if victims do not take them to court).

> 'The HSE's remit is much wider than safety at work. It oversees railway safety, licenses nuclear sites, regulates the chemical industry and deals with pesticides and explosives. The agency responsible for workers' safety naturally possesses the expertise needed to protect the public from the same risks. It proposes regulations and new law, and sets standards affecting almost all industrial processes and large segments of business.'
> The Times (8/12/94).

EU Health and Safety (First-Aid) Regulations 1981

Placed a duty on employers to ensure 'adequate first-aid provision for employees' – based on number of employees, distance from outside medical services, and whether work is high-risk. First-aid boxes, a first-aid representative with up-to-date training, a special room, and employee information, are required.

EU Control of Substances Hazardous to Health Directive 1988

Increased emphasis on prevention of exposure to carcinogens, with one report in the 1980s naming over 4,000 carcinogenic substances used by various industries. It required assessment of risk of exposure, replacement of the carcinogen if possible, reduction of the risk to as low a level as possible, emergency procedures, monitoring and health surveillance, and information and training provision.

Employment Act 1989

Supplemented existing law against sexual discrimination, in line with EU Equal Treatment Directive 1986, with the prevention of a pregnant woman working in environments which might endanger her unborn child being amongst the few discriminatory provisions allowed in the workplace.

EU Health and Safety Directives 1992

Came into force from 1st January 1993, after the HSE issued details of the new 'regulations' (!) to all organisations likely to be affected:

> *'Most of the duties in the new regulations are not completely new. They clarify and make more explicit what is current health and safety law. But there are some new approaches – especially in aspects of health and safety management, manual handling and use of display screens.'*

The new regulations cover six areas:

1 <u>M</u>anagement of health and safety at work regulations

Designed for a more systematic and better organised approach, and the HSE concluded that,

'Employers who have been thorough in their approach to their HSW Act duties should find the new regulations easy to get to grips with.' Employers are required to assess health and safety risks, plus consult with, and provide facilities for, employee health and safety representatives. There is also a reminder of employ<u>ees'</u> duty to comply, and report any risk or danger.

2 Provision and use of work <u>e</u>quipment regulations

Rationalised existing legislation and sought to improve protection of workers.

'In general, the regulations will make explicit what is already somewhere in the law or is good practice.' 'Work equipment' is defined as including a hand tool, e.g. a compressed-air driven drill, through to a complete refinery. 'Use' includes starting, stopping, repairing, modifying, installing, dismantling, programming, setting, transporting, maintaining, servicing and cleaning!

3 Manual <u>h</u>andling operations regulations

'The incorrect handling of loads causes large numbers of injuries and can result in pain, time off work and sometimes permanent disablement...', so these were designed to emphasise a modern, ergonomic approach. Employers are now required to carry out a risk assessment for all manual handling operations and reduce the danger, or even avoid it, where possible.

4 <u>W</u>orkplace (health, safety and welfare) regulations

Rationalised existing legislation, e.g. 1961 and 1963 Acts, and made clear employers' responsibilities for the working environment (e.g. lighting, ventilation, suitability of work stations, and seating), safety (e.g. windows and glazed doors to be of safety materials and marked, and floors not slippery or obstructed), facilities (e.g. drinking water, toilets, rest rooms for pregnant or nursing women, and rest areas with arrangements for no discomfort from tobacco smoke), and housekeeping (i.e. maintenance, equipment and facilities, cleanliness, and removal of waste).

5 <u>P</u>rotective equipment at work regulations

Covered selection, use (including relevant training) and maintenance of 'Personal Protective Equipment' – all equipment worn or held to protect against a risk to health or safety. *'PPE should be relied upon as a last resort. But where risks are not adequately controlled by other means you* [the employer] *will have a duty to ensure that suitable PPE is provided, free of charge, for employees exposed to these risks.'*

An important piece of (EU) legislation.

MEHWPS!

6 Display screen equipment work regulations

'Work with display screen equipment is not generally high risk, but it can lead to muscular and other physical problems [controversy in mid-1990s over 'Repetitive Strain Injury (RSI)'], *eye fatigue and mental stress. Problems of this kind can be overcome by good ergonomic design of equipment, furniture, the working environment and the tasks performed.'* Requirements of employers include provision of low-radiation and flicker-free computer monitors, breaks or changes of activity, and free eye tests for regular users of the equipment.

(c) Discrimination

Disability

Disabled Persons (Employment) Acts 1944 and 1958

Businesses employing 20 or more staff were required to employ a quota of registered disabled people. Thereafter employers could, and some did, discriminate with impunity. The *Employers' Forum on Disability*, trade unions and some MPs, finally pressured the [Conservative] Government into formulating more legislation.

Disability Discrimination Act 1995

Defined 'disability' as a physical or mental impairment with a substantial and long-term (12+ months) adverse effect on a person's ability to carry out day-to-day activities. From December 1996, employers were required to make 'reasonable' alterations to the workplace, reduce barriers to the disabled, and not discriminate in recruitment, training, promotion or dismissal. An estimated 2.5 million were affected, although 96% of businesses (with <20 employees) were still outside the scope of the legislation.

Sex

Equal Pay Act 1970

Stated that all employees have the right to treatment equal to that given to an employee of the opposite sex, if in the same employment, or doing similar work.

Sex Discrimination Act 1975

Made it illegal to discriminate on sexual grounds in matters of employment, training, redundancy and dismissal.

Sex Discrimination Act 1986

Said employers could set different retirement ages for men and women working in comparable employment.

EU European Pregnancy Directive 1992

Said it was unlawful to subject a woman to any detrimental treatment at work, e.g. dismissal, refusal of promotion or not offering training, because she is pregnant. All women are eligible for maternity leave of 14 weeks, regardless of length of service, or whether full-time or part-time. Afterwards, a woman can claim her old job.

Longer-term benefits for businesses too.

What does the word mean? (Means treating people differently/ worse.)

> *'Valerie Amos, the Chief Executive of the Equal Opportunities Commission, told the conference in Inverness that 87% of Britain's five million part-time workers were women, many of whom did not pay national insurance and were not entitled to unemployment or sickness payments. "20 years after the Equal Pay Act, women's full-time earnings are, on average, 79% of men's. When we look at part-time work it can be as low as 55%," she said.'*
>
> *The Times (30/10/93).*

> *'Sexual harassment can be defined as improper, offensive, and humiliating behaviour, practices or conduct which may threaten a person's job security, create an intimidating, unwelcoming and stressful work environment or cause personal offence and injury.'*
>
> *The Industrial Society (1993).*

EU Sexual Harassment Directive 1997

Drew a line between the protection of women's rights and political correctness, as part of a proposed package of new laws including stringent enforcement of existing ones on pay, promotion and protecting pregnant workers.

> *'54% of working women and 15% of working men experience sexual harassment. "I couldn't believe how bad some of the sexual harassment cases were. I was surprised how many men suffer from it – and suffer in silence. People should never do that."'*
>
> *Susan MacDonald, in Sex at Work, published by The Industrial Society (April 1998).*

White Paper 'Fairness at Work' 1998 said men as well as women would be allowed three months, parental leave when having a baby or adopting. Maternity leave would increase from 14 to 18 weeks in line with maternity pay.

Race

Race Relations Act 1976

Made it illegal to discriminate on grounds of racial origin in recruitment, employment, training, promotion or redundancy – complaint dealt with by an industrial tribunal, which may award compensation and order steps to prevent the discrimination.

> *'Group 4, the private security firm that runs two jails in England, has been found guilty of racially discriminating against a Sikh who applied for a job as a guard. The unanimous finding of the industrial tribunal in Croydon, was against the firm after the Indian-born man was refused a job but was invited for interview after reapplying under an assumed anglicised name [John Smith].'*
>
> *The Times (1/9/95).*

> *'A Muslim woman is suing the Body Shop for racial discrimination, claiming that it sacked her after she started to wear the hijab, a traditional Islamic headscarf.*
>
> *Body Shop spokeswoman Blair Palese said: "The Hounslow store was a franchise. We gave them policy and direction, but they are a separate company."'*
>
> *The Observer (26/1/97).*

(d) Data

Data Protection Act 1984

Stated that all organisations that held personal information, e.g. about employees, on their computers had to register as 'Data Users'.

Data must be:
- obtained fairly and lawfully
- for specified and lawful purposes
- relevant and sufficient only
- not held after the purpose has ceased
- accurate and kept up-to-date
- held securely.

Individuals can:
- ask if data about them is held
- have access, for a maximum fee of £10
- have incorrect data corrected or erased
- claim compensation for damage caused by incorrect data.

Marketing

There is no point in producing a good or service for which there is insufficient demand from likely customers to allow profit to be made, i.e. in highly competitive markets, production will need to be **market-led/consumer orientated**, rather than **product-led**.

Triumph, Norton, BSA, etc. were product-led.

- What was the main problem faced by British motorbike manufacturers, from the late 1960s (until the 1990s)?

Marketing finds out what consumers want and then attempts to meet those needs, at a profit.

It can also be defined as getting the right product to the right place at the right price at the right time. It is not the same as selling – that is making people buy what you've got. Marketing is making people want what you've got. It pays to know the market.

On what occasions is it important for an individual to market themselves effectively?

> 'The aim of marketing is to make selling superfluous. The aim is to know and understand the customer so well that the product or service sells itself.'
>
> Peter Drucker, US management guru (1974).

An organisation's Marketing Department will have the following functions:

- formulating **marketing objectives**, i.e. what the organisation hopes to achieve over a particular time period
- conducting **market research**, i.e. the collection of information for a database of potential customers
- composing a **marketing strategy**, using the database and including how to target likely customers, to achieve (shorter-term) objectives
- putting into effect the **marketing mix**, i.e. methods to be used
- **monitoring and modifying** the strategy and the mix, according to evidence from the market.

All marketing is targeted.

Advertising is only one section of this topic.

> 'Jaguar's new XK8 has been designed and crafted by women, and will be targeted at women by female Jaguar marketing executives. The company predicts that up to a quarter of all XK8s will be bought by women. The challenge has been to make this 300bhp, 4-litre, 32-valve V8 sports car "female-friendly" without turning it into a "girlie" car disdained by ego-fragile males.'
>
> The Times (2/3/96).

Marketing is concerned with **'adding value'**.

The marketing audit

This maps the current economic environment of the business, and how its situation is expected to change. The audit is likely to include:

Consider a range of goods and services, and how effective marketing adds value.

PEST Analysis – can be used by managers to assess the four types of constraint on their business [see Topic 4 Management and leadership]:

- **P**olitical
- **E**conomic
- **S**ocial
- **T**echnical.

Useful for coursework/ research assignment.

SWOT Analysis – can be used to assess the current market situation and the potential future situation [see Topic 4 Management and leadership]:

- **S**trengths
- **W**eaknesses
- **O**pportunities
- **T**hreats.

Michael Porter, in *Competitive Strategy: Techniques for Analysing Industries and Competitors* (1980), suggests five areas for assessing the competitive environment of a business:

- **Existing competition** – varies according to the maturity of the product-lifecycle (with greater competition for share of a mature market with static demand), **product differentiation** (with less competition if differentiated products appeal to different market segments), and **barriers to exit** (with specialist equipment being so expensive in 'capital-intensive' markets that costs of exiting are prohibitive).

- **New entrants** – depends on **barriers to entry** (e.g. high set-up costs, competing with existing marketing and brand loyalty, and possible trade barriers in foreign markets), and the response of existing competitors (e.g. 'limit- or predatory-' pricing).

- **Substitute products** – are there close substitutes? (e.g. building societies becoming close competition to banks in the 1980s, and artificial sweeteners competing with sugar).

- **Power of suppliers** – some essential raw materials or components only available from a limited number of suppliers, who thus wield significant **monopoly power**.

- **Power of buyers** – in an oligopoly (few sellers dominating) e.g. in food retailing, buyers have greater influence, particularly if large businesses able to achieve economies of scale (e.g. 'buying economies').

Marketing objectives

Possible conflict of objectives.

Objectives will need to be quantifiable, measurable and time-specific, and compatible with the organisation's overall objectives [see Topic 2 Objectives].

Igor Ansoff defined four marketing objectives for profitable growth, in *Corporate Strategy* (1965):

The Ansoff Matrix

Not to be confused with the Boston matrix.

	Present products	New products
Present markets	1 Market penetration	3 Product development
New markets	2 Market development/ extension	4 Diversification

1 **Market penetration** is when an existing product is given an increased market share or sales target in an existing market. New customers may be targeted, or the objective may be to sell more to existing customers.

2 **Market development** involves objectives of seeking and developing new markets, e.g. overseas, and new market segments. Some economies of scales may result in lower costs, but on the other hand there may be barriers to entry to some markets.

3 **Product development** will involve the often lengthy process of market research and then the development of new products which fill the gap, but also provide a suitable rate of return on the investment.

4 **Diversification** means going into markets and products that are new for the business (e.g. Mars taking over Pedigree Petfoods).

Analysing the market

E.g. for an exam case study, or a piece of research/ coursework.

A business has to analyse its market(s), continuously, and has to be market-led (rather than product-led). A 'market' can be defined as where buyers' demand meets producers' supply, and these two 'market forces' will determine the market price (or market-clearing price or the going-rate) for the particular good or service. There could also be government intervention, e.g. an increase in indirect taxation (e.g. VAT) to discourage the supply of a product, or a subsidy to encourage supply. [see Topic 10 External influences, p.113 The market].

Where does the expertise of each lie?

- Why does there need to be regular communication between the Marketing Department and the Production Department?

> 'CD-ROMS are being overtaken by sophisticated and flexible Internet software, leaving the main players such as the BBC and Dorling Kindersley fighting for space in a shrinking market.'
>
> The Times (22/1/98).

Market research

Use for your own coursework or piece of research.

The purpose is to provide information on the particular market to those managers responsible for the firm's marketing strategy, about what people want – a particular group of potential customers will need to be **targeted**.

Data can be:

- **Primary** – i.e. collected **for a specific purpose**. It will involve either a census (of every person in an area) or sampling (of a subset of the population).

or...

- **Secondary** – i.e. used **for another purpose** besides the original one. It could be internal data (from within the organisation, e.g. employee details or costings), or external data (e.g. from a government department, a newspaper, the TUC or the CBI).

and...

- **Quantitative** – i.e. in the form of **numbers**, e.g. showing the market share of different businesses, or the number of adults who will have seen a particular advertisement on television.

or...

- **Qualitative** – i.e. **without numbers**, e.g. giving the motives for customers buying, or not buying, a particular product.

Sampling

In most cases market research will involve choosing a sample to represent the whole **target group**. The larger the sample, the more accurate the results will be, but costs will also be greater – a full national census costs millions of pounds, e.g.

Random sampling is where every member of the target group/population has an equal chance of being chosen to provide responses. Computers might do the random selection.

Systematic sampling involves selecting, for example, every 10th item or person from a list of the target group (strictly speaking not in alphabetical order!).

Stratified sampling identifies distinguishable subgroups in the total group, then a certain number of members of each subgroup are chosen (at random).

Cluster sampling involves selecting a geographical area, and then *all* the members of that local group/population are sampled, e.g. a sample of small retailers in a particular town.

Convenience or opportunity sampling may be the most suitable type for small-scale research where time, finance and ability to travel are all limited. It involves choosing a relatively small sample of people who can be reached easily. The limitations of this type of sampling need to be acknowledged when the research is written up.

Quota sampling is the most commonly used type for market research, being relatively cheap and convenient. It is often used for election polls, for example. It involves choosing smaller groups or 'quotas' from the total population to be covered, with the skill of the researcher ensuring the quotas are representative, e.g. in terms of the sexes, age groups and...

Socio-economic groups

E.g. for an A level research assignment.

For targeting.

Consider the UK's national newspapers – which groups is each aimed at?

Group	Social status/class	Occupation	% of pop.	Examples
A	Upper middle	Higher managerial, professional or admin.	3.1	surgeon, company director
B	Middle	Middle managerial, professional or admin.	13.4	bank manager, head teacher
C1	Lower middle	Lower managerial etc., clerical, supervisory	22.3	bank clerk, teacher, nurse
C2	Skilled working	Skilled manual workers	31.2	joiner, electrician, welder
D	Working	Semi- and un-skilled manual workers	19.1	driver, postman, porter
E	Those at the lowest levels of the social structure	Low paid, and unemployed	10.9	pensioners, unemployed, casual and low-grade workers

Source: Policy Studies Institute (12/93).

Obtaining data

Desk research involves studying relevant documents such as reports from a local Chamber of Commerce (representing businesses in an area), from consultants specialising in trends in that market, or from the government (e.g. Department of Trade and Industry reports on trading in the Single Market). It may involve extrapolation from the data and analysing correlation, e.g. using scatter diagrams.

Field research involves getting data first-hand, for the specific purpose:

Again, useful for your own piece of research – the first you have done?

- **Interviews** can be formal or informal, and structured, unstructured or semi-structured.
- **Questionnaires** can include open or closed questions, depending on which type of responses are going to be most useful.
- **Testing panels** will be groups of consumers drawn from the targeted segment of the market, who will give their reactions to products and the marketing, e.g. the brand name, packaging and/or advertising.
- **Test/trial markets**, e.g. in a high-population urban area, to test the reactions of local consumers. Is the segment being successfully targeted?

Problems

- Is the data up-to-date?

- How is the data to be recorded?

- How can bias (e.g. of an interviewer and/or an interviewee) be eliminated or at least reduced?

- **Confidentiality** – how personal (and intrusive?) do the questions need to be? Will a business be concerned about some information (e.g. about finance) getting into the public domain?

- **Cross-referencing** between two or more sources of data, can provide proof of the reliability of the information, but it may not always be possible.

The marketing mix

This is how the marketing will be put into effect.

The 4P's: (a) product

A product can be a good or service. In competitive markets, businesses have to be customer-driven. They may use types of **product differentiation** (e.g. package design and/or a brand name) in an attempt to convince potential customers that their good or service *is* different from competitors' products.

There may be an emphasis on what the business believes is a **unique selling point (USP)** for its product. A single-product business may be more vulnerable to market forces [see Topic 10 External influences], so risks could be spread by devising a product plan which includes a portfolio of products – **the product mix**. This diversification could be planned so that products are at different stages of their **life-cycle**. A well-balanced portfolio will allow well-established products to finance development of new products.

In 1970 the Boston Consulting Group (BCG) published a model of how businesses should plan their product mix, for future profitability:

The Boston Matrix

Four types of products

		Relative market share	
		high	low
Market growth rate	high	Star	Problem child
	low	Cash cow	Dog

(i) Star

- High share of a market in the 'growth' stage of the product life-cycle.
- Requires significant injections of capital to finance the rapid growth.
- May have negative cashflows but seen as having **potential** for high sales, and profit.

E.g. Proctor and Gamble's 'Pampers' nappies became an almost instant 'star' in the early 80s.

(ii) Cash cow

- High market share, bringing in high sales revenue, cashflows and (usually) profit.
- No market growth likely.
- Product may have a personality/image in the market.
- The large amounts of cash brought in can be used to subsidise 'stars'.

E.g. Some brands of toothpaste, if the market is unlikely to grow.

(iii) Problem child

- Low share of a market with high potential for growth.
- Relatively large injections of finance needed (as with 'stars').
- Uncertainty about future sales revenue, cashflow and profit.
- Decision needed on whether or not to halt production, or (if possible) to sell a brand.

But could become a 'star', *or...*

(iv) Dog

- Not going anywhere – no growth potential.
- Any profit has to be reinvested just to maintain market share.
- Identify and remove from the product portfolio.

But, the BCG said, management may be reluctant to get rid of 'dogs' because:

- sentimental attachment (due to links with origins or image of the business)
- falling sales and profits being blamed on other causes
- searching for (non-existent?) 'extension strategies'
- managers unwilling to be reassigned
- and/or preoccupation with new products (preventing decisions on 'dogs').

Possible criticisms of the Boston Matrix

For evaluation.

- An oversimplification and too narrow, including only two main factors.
- Current market share may not indicate future prospects for market share.
- High growth markets may lack size or stability (e.g. if in fashion).
- No account is taken of the marketing expertise available.
- No account is taken of fit between products and the business's capabilities.
- Perhaps borrow working capital rather than rely on cash generation.
- Longer-term profit might be higher priority than short-term cashflows?
- Will products in high growth markets always need more cash?
- Will products with high market shares always generate the cash – depends?
- Other significant factors may include:
  - efficiency and abilities of managers
  - product innovation
  - corporate image
  - capital- or labour- intensity
  - social and legal pressures perhaps including ethics [see Topic 10 External influences].

Product life-cycle

Products, like people, have a life-cycle, i.e. the length of time over which it appeals to customers – a few months or even hundreds of years...

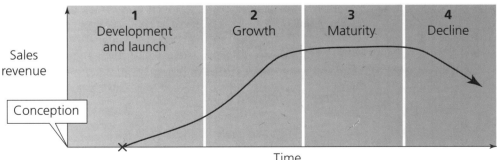

What would happen to the cashflow – negative until some time in the growth stage?

1 **Development and launch** – R and D, market research, and (if the product thought to be 'commercial') a launch on to the market. The riskiest stage of the life-cycle, with relatively high costs and relatively low return/revenue from sales, sometimes called 'the Death Valley Ride', because of the negative cashflows!

2 **Growth** – the product establishes itself in the market, and may become easier to sell (e.g. to wholesalers)? Advertising can become more *persuasive* than *informative*. Increasing competition, perhaps from new entrants, may force down the price.

3 **Maturity** – sales revenue reaches a peak. Increased advertising may be necessary to protect/maintain the market share. This stage may last for a relatively long period [see *extension strategies* below], when the product will hopefully make the biggest profits and justify all the previous expenditure invested in it. More competitors entering the market may drive it towards saturation.

4 **Decline** – sales start to fall as the product comes to be viewed as old-fashioned, old-technology and/or obsolete. It may be a 'cash cow' [see p. 59 Boston Matrix], or even withdrawn if it might affect the image of the business and the launch of new products.

> 'John Hale, Chairman of the family-owned Golden Bear Co. Ltd that gave children Mr. Men, Postman Pat and Forever Friends toys, says he is also working on Teletubbie hug-me backpacks and a full Homehill playset complete with Noo-Noos the friendly vacuum cleaner from Tellytubbieland. The company is now working on the prototype for Talking Teletubbies, which will be unveiled at the British Toy and Hobby Fair at Olympia in January [1998]...
>   Richard Perks, of the retail researchers and analysts "Verdict", said that, like all merchandise, Teletubbies had a life cycle and the manufacturers were taking care to elongate it as much as possible. "Parents might be depressed about this, but it is the market", he said. "Investors will want a return on their investment. In five years' time no one will want Teletubbies so they have to be careful not to accelerate its life cycle."'
>
>   *The Times* (8/12/97).

Managing the product life-cycle

The key to achieving long-term profits from products is in forecasting the trend and duration of each stage of the life-cycle. The **marketing mix** might be changed, to inject new life into a product, either to increase the growth stage or to form an **extension strategy**, to arrest or at least delay the decline stage.

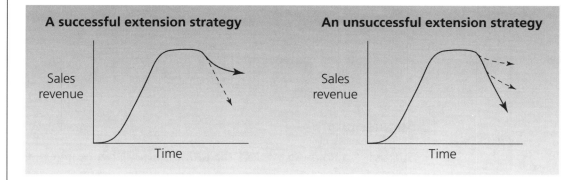

Consider an example for each of these.

E.g.
- The 'Lux' brand of soap is over 90 years old!

Madonna's brand image, apparently in the mature stage of its product life-cycle, was relaunched in the mid-90s. Her record company claimed that her new album, *Bedtime Stories*, signalled 'a new, bright, clean, clear and mellow approach, with an increased emphasis on song-orientated rhythm and blues'. She has since been the lead in the film *Evita* and launched more music.

Other examples? What is 'a one-hit wonder'?

> 'As an unbelievably famous person you are only allowed to operate with everyone's approval for a limited amount of time.'
>
>   Madonna, in interview with US journalist Norman Mailer (1994).

New products

- **Innovative products** – a need identified, and not yet satisfied, e.g. a cure for a type of cancer, or the introduction of the compact disc (CD).
- **Significant adaptations** – existing products in a different format, e.g. freeze-dried coffee, or 'draught' widgets in beer cans.
- **Imitative, 'copycat'** or **'me-too'** products – copies of existing products, but legal if not infringing Intellectual Property laws [see Topic 7 Operations management] e.g. red-and-white cola cans, or copies of fashion designs.
- **Simulated adaptations** – no technical change involved but consumers believe them to be different e.g. Mars' 'Marathon' chocolate bar becoming 'Snickers' (1990), or 'Opal Fruits' to 'Starburst' (1998), or 'car badge engineering'.

It has been estimated that eight out of ten new products fail within a year – so there are risks involved. A new product might be introduced to:
- change the product mix, i.e. number of product lines
- change the depth of the product mix, i.e. number of products in a line
- reposition the product mix, i.e. taking it up- or down-market
- change the emphasis of the line within the product mix
- allow further segmentation of the market [see Segmentation below].

Success may depend on the product being:
- user-friendly, ergonomically designed and perhaps not too complex
- competitive or superior to the competition on quality or price
- a good fit in with current lifestyles
- suitable for sales promotions, e.g. free samples
- marketed effectively, so potential customers are aware of its benefits.

Failure may result from:
- a change in tastes/fashion
- actual costs higher than standard costs [see Topic 7 Operations management, p. 78 Costs of production]
- problems of quality/reliability
- retaliation by competitors...how?
- ineffective marketing, perhaps including price decisions [see p. 57 Pricing].

Segmentation

Successful marketing involves **targeting** particular consumers, and market research can be used to segment a market, i.e. break it down into groups according to gender, age, race, creed, geographical area, or **socio-economic groups** [see p. 57 Sampling].

> 'The number of single-person households is set to rise from 6.8 million in 1995 to 8 million by the end of the century, according to a survey by Mintel [a market research company]. The survey found that single people under 55 have on average 8 hours a week more leisure time than their counterparts in households of two or more, and more than 60% usually eat in front of the TV.
>
> *The Observer* (24/3/96).

> 'According to "Automotive News" in the US, the Japanese company is now targeting lesbians, running ads which endearingly say: "It loves camping, dogs and long-term commitment. Too bad it's only a car."'
>
> *The Times* (27/3/96).

'Business' means taking risks!

An example.

An example.

E.g. all television adverts are targeted – check on a few.

Pronounced 'nitch' by some Americans.

Can you find any examples for either?

- **Niche marketing** means finding a segment of a market which can be targeted as its own (usually smaller) specialised market, and which as yet is not (wholly) catered for.

- **Fragmentation** can become a marketing problem, and is where a market is split up into too many segments for any to provide substantial profits.

Branding

A brand is a name, term, sign, symbol/logo, or design used to identify a supplier's good or service and for **product differentiation**, i.e. encouraging consumers to believe that the product is different from the competition (even though, in some markets, there are few differences between the competing products).

Consumers must believe the product is different – even unique. That 'USP' again!

- **Individual product branding** – used to distinguish products within the product line of a business, e.g. types of washing powder, targeted at different (albeit overlapping) segments of the market.

- **Family branding** – where a business name, e.g. belonging to a famous food company, is attached to a whole range of diversified products.

- **Line branding** – for a particular product line, e.g. a famous cola company having a range of colas, e.g. cherry, pizza, diet, caffeine-free etc.

- **Own brands** – increasingly common, e.g. where large food retailers have their own-brand products on the shelves next to the premium brands.

Branding is used to:

Can you find any examples for these?

- aid **consumer recognition**, where the brand name is used as a focus for all promotional activities

- allow **product differentiation**, to reduce price competition (e.g. in 'Cola Wars' after 1994)

- generate **brand loyalty**, to enhance repeat sales e.g. of FMCGs

- allow possible **brand-stretching**, e.g. being used for a new (in 1994) washing-up liquid.

NB The dangers of **brand-vandalism**, i.e. where a new product might harm the image of the brand name, e.g. a famous motorcycle brand being used for down-market products.

and... **brand-cannibalism**, i.e. where the new product becomes a competitor to an earlier product from the same business, e.g. new items of confectionery or chewing gum.

Do you go in for 'conspicuous consumption'?

> 'The market in the 1990s will be much more difficult than it was in the late 1980s. The consumer will be more focused on real, intrinsic value rather than on conspicuous consumption. The strong brands that do stand for something will get stronger. The prize will go to those people with really good brands who run their businesses highly effectively and totally focused on the consumer.'
> Tony Greener, Chairman of Guinness, in *The Sunday Times* (8/12/91).

Branding may not work successfully where consumers consider the products to be all the same – **homogeneous**, e.g. some vegetables and fruit.

Brands have to be managed, requiring considerable marketing effort and expense. Some have become so famous that they end up as the generic name for the product, e.g. a Hoover, a Coke, or a Biro. This might be a disadvantage, if the branding is not differentiating the product, i.e. if consumers use the generic name but will accept other brands of the product.

The USP!

E.g.

Müller Yoghurt was launched in 1988. By 1991 it was a 'star' [see p. 59 Boston matrix], showing an 81% growth in its market in that year. The Unique Selling Point (USP) was the separation of fruit and yoghurt, allowing consumers to vary the taste of each mouthful, and with a fifth more content than the current main brands. The 'Ski' brand led the market before Muller changed the rules – from upright pots and the belief that consumers would not pay a premium, e.g. for creaminess.

Packaging

Consider examples of each.

In the 1930s, before the arrival of plastics, several food products, e.g. butter, bacon and biscuits, were sold loose. By 1995 the packaging business was worth nearly £9 billion, with many different types of packaging and materials in use. Packaging has often become a very important part of the product:

- for protection and convenience – in transport, storage, display and handling, for the manufacturer, wholesaler

- as part of the marketing mix – including the trade mark, logo, colours and/or design, to attract customers and regenerate sales, e.g. for FMCGs. The packaging may also be seasonal.

- to assist product performance – (not only in the profit-generating sense but) in physical operation, e.g. soap dispensers or aerosols.

Some types of packaging may raise ethical issues [see Topic 10 External influences, p. 111 Ethics] e.g. on the question of disposability and the environment.

The 4P's: (b) place/distribution

Making goods available to users/consumers involves two main decisions:

- **Method of transport** – Depends on the type of goods, e.g. high-bulk/low-value like sand, or low-bulk/high-value like human organs, and the location of production [see Topic 7 Operations management, p. 73 Location]. There will be several factors, e.g. most rail journeys also involving road transport, and whether a business should have its own fleet of road vehicles.

- **Channel of distribution** – The procedure, or 'channel management' required to get a product to the customers. The traditional channel includes using the wholesaler, but there are other possible channels.

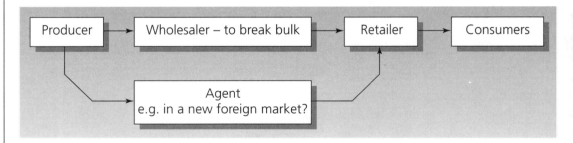

Agents develop expertise in particular products or markets, and offer professional marketing services that would be expensive for a business to provide for itself, e.g. a foreign market may have possible cultural, language and/or currency barriers to trade. Agents do not take title/ownership to the products, and are usually paid **commission** according to the value of sales.

Wholesalers' main function is to 'break bulk' between the mass production of manufacturers/suppliers (or importing agent) and the smaller quantities required by retailers. Large retail chains buy large quantities direct from manufacturers, missing out the middleman and that mark-up.

Retailers buy from manufacturers or wholesalers and sell to consumers/end-users. They range in size from a market stall to the large food retail chains (e.g. Tesco's, Sainsbury's, etc.). 'Loss-leaders' are used, but the mark-up on most products provides the profits.

- Direct selling to consumers may mean lower costs for the manufacturer and so a lower price for the consumer, e.g. furniture at direct-from-the-factory prices. Mail order is the fastest growing form of UK retailing.

Marketing abroad

Trade agreements (e.g. GATT) and trading blocs (e.g. The Single Market), and better communications generally, have reduced **barriers to trade** (e.g. currencies, language differences and documentation), and have made it easier for most types of business which have reasons to enter a foreign market.

- Growth may be low, or zero, in the domestic market. The risks [see Topic 2 Objectives] and likely rates of return [see Topic 9 Finance, p. 109 Ratios] will have to be weighed up, perhaps using external consultants.

- Economies of scale may be increased because of the increased volume of sales generated, and provide a competitive advantage.

- Competition in the domestic market (from foreign companies) may encourage a business to seek other markets in order to survive. Improvements in communications, including the Internet, have made buyers more aware of global markets.

A checklist for a business launching its products abroad

- **Size of the market** being considered – What per cent currently imported?
- **Political and economic stability of the market** – The Department of Trade and Industry (DTI) runs the government's Export Initiative, including advice for exporters. Further advice available from an Area Advisory Group of the British Overseas Trade Board (BOTB).
- **Growth trends of the market** – Production and consumption.
- **Current products in the market** – Satisfying the market? ...Room for more products?...a 'niche market' identifiable?
- **Market leaders** – Their shares of the market, marketing methods and services offered.
- **Possible channels of distribution** – The costs of each.
- **Legal requirements**, including documents, e.g. import licences and for product standards for a non-Single Market country.
- **Tariffs** (i.e. import taxes) **or quotas** – (i.e. restrictions on import volume).
- **Transport** aspects – Speed, frequency and cost.

A business might consider setting up its own subsidiary – involved in the whole process from production design through to marketing to customers, or concentrating on a particular role, e.g. marketing, in that country.

> 'The newly announced sponsorship of the Volvo China Golf Tour and Volvo China Open is an important aspect of the company's long-term marketing strategy...in a country predicted to be the World's biggest economy by 2020.'
>
> *Volvo Magazine (9/95).*

> 'Tesco, the supermarket group, has made its boldest move into Eastern Europe with the purchase of businesses in the Czech Republic and Slovakia for £77 m...the Czech Republic's GDP is forecast to grow at more than 4% this year, and Slovakia's is forecast to grow 5%.'
>
> *The Times (6/3/96).*

'Location' not so crucial for this retailing?

Will the Single Currency help exporters in the EU? – see p. 131.

Do you know another country very well?

Expensive but under direct control.

Getting in early!

The 4P's: (c) pricing

'A cynic is a man who knows the price of everything and the value of nothing.'
Oscar Wilde

Setting the right price for a product is a crucial aspect of marketing. A 'price plateau' represents the price which the potential customers would consider appropriate at that particular time, i.e. the going rate, and this exists for most products. If a product is considered over-priced it will be perceived as poor value for money, and little will be purchased. If it is under-priced the attitude 'You get what you pay for!' may apply, with quality being perceived as low. Again, sales could be disappointingly low.

There are short- and long-term objectives to be considered when pricing goods or services [see Topic 2 Objectives] e.g. survival may become the priority in a recession, and imply low prices to maintain some sales and cashflow. Larger businesses may even be able to suffer losses in order to maintain a market share, to ensure longer-term survival. On the other hand, the avoidance of a price war may be the main priority, because the business would be put under pressure by the market leaders [see p. 67 Limit or predatory pricing]. Markets often have fairly common prices, with businesses following market leaders and using non-price competition methods [see p. 67, Promotion]. Gauging price elasticity of demand will be important. [see Topic 10 External influences, p. 114].

Is a market 'fair'? How do you decide?

Economic theory assumes that a price will be determined by **market forces** reaching an equilibrium [see Topic 10 External influences, p. 113 The economic environment: (a) The market]. A business may simply have to try and match the market price/going-rate for its products, or may have some control over its prices.

Economic theory also suggests a firm will use revenue and cost data to calculate the output and price that will **maximise profits** (where MC = MR). As we have just seen, a business may have other priorities, and there are several possible pricing methods:

New product

- **Price skimming** – where a high/premium price is set for a new product, e.g. a new computer games console, in order to 'skim the cream', i.e. targeting a market segment with relatively inelastic demand, in which customers are prepared to pay extra. The price can be reduced once the product is established.

- **Penetration pricing** – where a low price is set, to break into a market, gain a particular share and build consumer loyalty. A price rise may be possible later.

Costs

- **Cost-plus pricing**, or **mark-up** – where standard costs are calculated and then a certain percentage is added on. High stock turnover, e.g. for large food retail chains, can allow a relatively low percentage mark-up. However, a seaside gift shop might need a higher mark-up – sometimes as much as 100%.

Often included in exam questions.

- **Contribution cost pricing** – where only the additional or **marginal costs** are included, i.e. only those direct costs attributable to the production and marketing of the particular product. Then a percentage mark-up is added to give the price to be charged to customers, so that the production will at least make a 'contribution' to the indirect costs as well. In this way, a business might accept an order for its product although the price does not cover the total costs – an overall loss. [see Topic 7 Operations management, p. 78 Types of costing].

NB It may be better to accept the order (rather than lose an important customer for the future). Only a proportion of sales can be on the basis of lower-price/contribution-to-indirect costs otherwise the business cannot be in overall profit!

Break-even analysis may be used by a business to examine the implications of several different costs-based pricing scenarios [see Topic 7 Operations management, p. 81 Costs (c)].

Demand

- **Life-cycle pricing** – according to the **current or expected demand** for the product, e.g. the price may be raised if the product is at the growth stage of the product life-cycle (before maturity).

- **Price discrimination** – division of a market into sub-markets, only possible if each has a different **price elasticity of demand**, e.g. airline travel divided into 'first class', 'executive/business class', 'tourist class' etc., each segment targeted at different customers and with different pricing.

Competition

(e.g. for launching a new product)

- **Competitive pricing** – monitoring and following the market leaders' prices, being careful not to undercut and spark off a cut-throat **price war**.

- **Limit or predatory pricing** – possible for a business with monopoly power/influence in the market, to discourage new competitors. Unmatchable prices can be raised once the competitive threat is reduced.

- **Promotion pricing** – used in the maturity phase of a product's life-cycle, to maintain market share. It may take the form of a price reduction or giving more of the product for the same price, e.g. 12% extra.

- **Prestige pricing** – setting a higher or 'premium' price for a good or service at the top of its product portfolio, e.g. for a top-of-the-range car. There may be a limited customer base, but the status of the product, and even the range of branded products, might be enhanced.

In practice, businesses may use a variety of the above methods to set the **base prices** for their products.

The following are all types of prices...Wages, salaries, fees, commission, tenders, bids, cash and trade/bulk discounts, estimates and quotations, 'direct from the factory', 'APR'.

> 'British Airways has sparked a price war with the Eurostar rail service to Paris and Brussels by slashing air fares [to £59] to both cities...30% lower than Eurostar's cheapest return. Eurostar started the operation on November 14th last year and on May 23rd passed the 1 million passenger mark...A BA spokesman denied its prices were in response to Eurostar.'
>
> The Times (1/6/95).

> 'Stena [ferries] has launched the first salvo in what may prove the most savage price war yet. Bookings made before March 31 on some of its summer night-time crossings have been discounted by 40%, allowing a car and up to 8 passengers to sail for as little as £129...A second front in the price war has been opened up in the cross-Channel duty-free shops. Eurotunnel is now offering 66% off high street spirits and tobacco brands. Stena has retaliated with a range of keenly priced duty-free offers. Only P&O has remained loftily above the fray, insisting it does not need the help of cut-price artificial stimulants to tempt passengers on to its ships...'
>
> The Times (5/4/96).

The 4P's: (d) promotion

The overall objective of promotion is ensuring the survival and growth of a business through an increase in long-term demand for its product(s). Selling will be the outcome of successful promotion, which will try to achieve several of the following:

How many market 'wars' have you come across? – 'Store wars', 'Bar wars', 'Cola wars' plus...?

Where would each be found?

Examples of each?

- inform and 'energise' potential consumers
- persuade a wholesaler or retailer to stock the good
- encourage continuing purchases
- widen and deepen the total market
- enter a new market segment
- introduce new products
- maintain or increase market share
- enlarge the total market
- counteract prejudice
- offset marketing efforts of competitors
- build goodwill for the business and its products
- offset damage to the business's image by an incident
- capitalise on a fortunate incident or relationship
- participate in a joint/co-operative venture.

Will consumers *believe* the product is different, even 'unique'?

Easy to remember.

A I D A !   Get the **A**ttention of targeted consumers

Tell them more, to get them **I**nterested

Encourage greater interest, towards **D**esire

Energise potential consumers to take **A**ction

The promotion mix ... five elements

(a) Advertising

Again, this is important, but is only one part of the promotion mix!

To communicate a chosen message to a targeted audience so as to change their behaviour in a predicted and desired way.

Often referred to as 'above the line promotion', advertising can be:

- competitive
- generic
- point-of-sale
- soft-sell

- informative
- corporate
- direct mail
- 'Generation X'!

- persuasive
- classified
- subliminal.

Advertising can be used for:

- **Creating primary demand** – when a new product is introduced to the market. Credibility and reliability may need to be established.

- **Creating brand preference** – particularly during the growth stage of the product's life-cycle, with emphasis on the product's USP.

- **Increasing market share** – achieved by encouraging potential purchasers to compare the product. Could be used when preparing the maturity stage.

'Virgin boss Richard Branson has been forced to drop a national newspaper advertising campaign [for a 'Virgin Direct' Personal Equity Plan (PEP)] after a legal threat from the Bradford and Bingley Building Society, who warned that unless Virgin stopped making fun of its bowler hat trademark, it would take action for alleged infringement...'
Mail on Sunday (22/10/95).

- **Maintaining market share** – defending product sales from the competition possibly a counter-move, when sales level out in the maturity stage.

- **Entering new markets or segments** – to introduce the product to potential consumers.
- **Reinforcing demand** – keeping the product's name in the minds of consumers perhaps during the maturity stage.

Decisions are required about which advertising media would be most effective, with due regard to the expense involved, e.g. on television – the most widely seen medium in the UK.

Types of media include:
- independent television – national and regional; satellite, cable and terrestrial
- independent radio – national and local
- newspapers – national, regional and local
- cinema
- billboards/posters
- motor racing vehicles
- hot-air balloons
- soccer, rugby, cricket, tennis kit and merchandise.

> *In April 1998 Manchester United announced 'Football Club' will be dropped from the official badge, 'because everyone knows it's a football club'.*

There are controls on advertising (besides specific ones on alcohol, tobacco, pornography, '18' films) e.g.:

Written – **Advertising Standards Authority (ASA)** issued and monitors the 'British Code of Advertising Practice' and can ban advertisements or campaigns after responding to complaints from the public.

Television – **Independent Television Commission (ITC)** issued its own 'Code of Practice' and can investigate complaints and ban advertisements.

In both cases, businesses often consult them before an advertisement is used or a campaign launched, because they do not want to waste money and/or attract any image-damaging publicity. (On the other hand some businesses might welcome being banned for the extra publicity it brings.)

> *'The problem for marketers is that "ABs" [see p. 58, Socio-economic groups] are notoriously hard to reach with advertising. They watch just two-thirds the average amount of commercial television, and they are often fiercely resistant to its blandishments.'*
>
> *The Times (17/4/96).*

(b) Personal selling

This includes any **face-to-face communication** (except retailing, which is normally analysed separately) designed to inform or persuade a potential customer. Sales people may be graduates, technically qualified and/or well-trained, and so relatively expensive to use.

Related costs may include a company car, commission on top of a basic salary, travel and hotel expenses, and expenses for entertaining potential customers, but personal selling may be very effective for selling technical or complex products. It may:

- gain new customers – focusing on those more likely to buy
- increase sales – more careful attention to the customer's needs
- deal with customer dissatisfaction/complaints – to maintain good relations with important customers
- open up new segments – after careful targeting based on detailed market research
- give specialist technical support, e.g. for PCs, to add value to the product.

Can you think of others? What costs are involved?

(c) Sales promotion

Consider examples of each.

This consists of any incentives to potential customers to buy now rather than later, or deciding against buying at all, e.g.:

- using 'new' labels
- price reductions
- vouchers/free gifts
- special offers

- free samples
- coupons
- trial offers
- in-store demonstrations.

- limited editions
- competitions
- retailers' discount

Sales promotion can be used to:

- launch a new product – with incentives to try it
- increase the level of demand – at least short-term
- maintain market share – to offset competitors' marketing
- bring more people into a shop – e.g. using 'Sale' signs and tags
- get more retailers' shelf-space – boosted sales may lead to bigger (stock) order
- encourage wholesalers to buy more stock – also encouraging retailers.

(d) Publicity

> 'Any publicity is better than no publicity!'

That depends, but publicity can be used to:

- create an image – to enhance the status of the firm in its potential market
- inform potential consumers – otherwise unaware?
- publicise progress – e.g. innovation, creating consumer confidence, and also aiding recruitment [see Topic 5 Human resource management, p. 29 Recruitment]
- raising workers' morale – e.g. by highlighting their achievements.

How would you go about the task?...and for your part of the world?

> In April 1998 Robin Cook, the Foreign Secretary, named 33 experts who would form 'Panel 2000' and have the task of transforming Britain's global image. Members included Sir Colin Marshall (chairman of BA and President of the CBI), top designer Stella McCartney, Channel 4 presenter Zeinab Badawi, (new) Cabinet Minister Peter Mandelson, athlete Judy Simpson, and Martin Bell MP. Mr Cook told the media that, 'We do not reject our heritage – we value our heritage. But we also need to be a forward-looking country prepared to face the challenges of the new millennium. It is important that we all project a positive image of our work and of the modern Britain abroad.'

Some firms have their own **Public Relations (PR)** department, or they hire an outside specialist firm. Either way, PR can play an important role in building the chosen image of the organisation, and may involve:

- Deciding on the type of publicity – with some 'free publicity', e.g. in newspapers and magazines, still incurring costs for the firm involved.

- Corporate relations – ensuring the appropriate image to business customers is built, then maintained. Corporate hospitality, e.g. invitations to a film premiere, a box at the opera or a sports ground, or a lunch (with some famous guests) might be expensive, but considered worthwhile in terms of the long-term image.

- Identifying specific interest groups – whose activities might relate to those of the business, e.g. schoolchildren.

- Media relations – using the press or television to attract attention to an aspect of the business, e.g. a new product, or a takeover attempt (e.g. to encourage the other company's shareholders to sell shares).

- Lobbying politicians – to influence legislation and government departments on matters of direct relevance to the business.
- Charitable donations – creating a favourable public image.
- A Customer Relations Department – to handle enquiries and complaints.
- Sponsorship – of appropriate people and/or events, e.g. in art or sport.

> "Coronation Street" is to be sponsored by Cadbury's in a £10 million deal. Cadbury's name will appear in the opening and closing credits of the programme and the company will have the right to attach the "Coronation Street" name to its products in special promotions..."Coronation Street" is regularly watched by 18 million viewers.'
>
> The Times (27/3/96).

> 'Sponsors' logos on the kits of top English football clubs are being taken over by high-tech companies as the new affluent breed of football fan changes the face of the game...Packard Bell, the American home computing company, will join names such as JVC, Sharp and Hewlett Packard on Premiership shirts after signing a sponsorship deal worth about £4 million with Leeds United. Senior company and football officials said the deal was part of an unstoppable trend, ending more than 100 years of football's working-class, beer-swilling image.'
>
> The Times (24/4/96).

(e) Direct marketing

This refers to the promotion where individual approaches are made to customers – a growing type of promotion, apparently because:
- career women have little time for shopping
- parking problematic in some cities
- some unwillingness to queue at checkouts
- leisure time regarded as increasingly important.

Main direct marketing methods involve:
- mail order catalogues
- electronic shopping
- television marketing
- video marketing
- direct (junk) mail
- the Internet.

What are the attractions of the Net – to users? ...to advertisers.

Operations management

'Production' means any process which adds **value** to a good or service.
Value can be added to a good or service in two ways:

Marketing – There are various techniques used to persuade the customer that the product has the extra value worth paying for [see Topic 6 Marketing] e.g. a famous branded cola.

OM/Production – Putting raw materials through a process to make them more valuable, i.e. the final assembled product will be of more use and value, than the total of the inputs, e.g. an engine of a famous car manufacturer.

In Accounting terms, 'added value' is the revenue from goods and services a business provides to others *minus* the costs of the goods and services the business buys from others. This can also be called **gross profit** [see Topic 9 Finance] of the business, and will be used to pay expenses, taxes and dividends, as well as some being 'retained', i.e. reinvested/ploughed back.

Consider examples of adding value in both ways.

Kanban see p. 85.

Methods of production

	Job ...'one-off':	**Batch** ...'a few at a time':	**Flow** ...'many at a time'
Example products	A house, painting, hand-made pottery, customised car, special wedding cake.	A small housing estate, Morgan cars, sheds, small bakery, or brewery.	Matches, lightbulbs, cigarettes, cola, some cars, some beer, pins, computer chips.
Labour needed	Usually labour-intensive, with high skill and craftsmanship involved.	More division of labour, perhaps with less skill required from each individual.	Extensive division of labour, often extended to automation (and redundancies).
Levels of stocks	Ordered as required, so minimal level.	Larger stocks needed, probably for several batches (e.g. yeast for bread).	Large stocks needed to maintain production flow, unless JIT used [see p.85 Stocks].
Unit cost (AC)	Relatively high (e.g. for an individual product made to order).	Some economies of scale lower AC. Larger batches more economic.	Extensive economies of scale Æ lowest AC – efficiency.
Other info.	The cheapest to set up.	Larger batches not always possible.	Mass production only viable if sufficient market demand. Expensive to set up.

The method adopted will depend on:
- the nature and variety of the products
- the size and frequency of customers' orders
- the stage of development of the enterprise
- the stage of development of the host economy, determining the technology, and the availability and prices of capital and labour.

Cell production

- First used in USSR in 1950s.
- Machines not grouped according to function.
- Machines grouped together according to the family of components they produce.
- Simplifies production flows, with errors spotted more quickly.
- Faster feedback from the next cell – the customer.

Lean production

- 'Lean production is lean because it aims to use less of everything compared with mass production' – John Krafcik, researcher at Massachusetts Institute of Technology (MIT), and first to coin the phrase (in 1984).
- $5 million five-year study of world car industry undertaken at MIT – to compare 'benchmarking' Japanese production techniques with USA and Europe's, after concern about increasing market shares gained by Japanese vehicles.
- Significant differences found…

> 'The EC car industry will have to sacrifice jobs, cut working hours, and introduce new training methods if it is to compete with US and Japanese manufacturers, the EC's Industry Commissioner, Mr Martin Bangemann, said yesterday. He urged the industry to invest in new plants with the aim of creating a European "lean production" system as productive and cost-efficient as the Japanese equivalent.'
>
> Financial Times (10/11/93).

E.g. less stocks with JIT Kanban.

An economy's production can be divided into…

Primary	Getting the raw materials – 'extraction'	mining, farming, fishing, forestry, oil exploration
Secondary	Processing the raw materials – 'manufacturing' and 'construction'	oil refining, vehicle manufacture, house-building, Channel Tunnel building
Tertiary	Different types of services [including 'commerce']	tourism, banking, insurance, health services, advertising, transport services, telecommunications

Location

A mail order business might have much more choice about location (if there is an efficient postal service). For most businesses, choice is restricted. For retailers it is said there are three crucial aspects: 'Location, location… and location!'

Other businesses have to consider several factors:

- Closeness to sources of raw materials – e.g. for a bulk-decreasing industry, where the finished product is relatively less bulky and easier to transport than the raw materials or components.
- Closeness to the market – e.g. for a bulk-increasing industry, where the raw materials are relatively less bulky and easier to transport than the finished product.
- Other communication aspects – e.g. for businesses requiring access to a certain type of transport (e.g. an airport, for speed), or no problems with mobile phone signals, or

ready access to certain IT facilities (e.g. via an Internet server). Teleworking has meant some workers can operate long distances from the central work location, perhaps from home.

- Suitable labour available – e.g. an electronics company requiring a local pool of skilled manual workers. Other businesses may be able to use labour from further afield, or may be more capital-intensive and so require a relatively small workforce.

> '27% of UK firms, large and SMEs [Small to Medium Enterprises], plan to relocate by the year 2000.'
>
> From a survey by Black Horse Relocation Ltd (9/95).

- **Planning permission** – e.g. a local council allowing 'change of use' for a particular building, or easing planning restrictions to encourage businesses to locate in an area needing regeneration and more jobs, or refusing it in a rural Conservation Area.
- **Government incentives** – e.g. tax allowances and fewer planning restrictions to encourage businesses to relocate in (one of 26) 'Enterprise Zones' – centres of high unemployment. Grants for buildings and equipment, soft loans (lower interest rates), and subsidies for training workers, may be available for businesses which locate in a 'Development Area', for example.

Multinationals

International companies sell products in several countries.

Multinationals have production facilities in other countries besides their home base. Particularly since the mid-1980s, several foreign multinationals have located production in the UK.

- New **m**arkets, e.g. 'a gateway to Europe'/the EU – with no tariff barriers on EU products (e.g. Toyota cars made in Derby).
- **E**conomies of scale – from the expanded overall output, or from concentrating all the production of a particular component (e.g. car engines) on one site.
- A pool of **l**abour – from the redundancies from traditional industries, and workers who may accept relatively low wages or may have required skills.
- Lower **t**axes – e.g. Corporation Tax (on business profit) may be relatively low. 'Transfer pricing' means organising prices of raw materials so that the value is added, and the profit made, in the country where the tax is lowest.
- Central and local **g**overnment help – e.g. giving easier planning permission and grants to provide jobs and training in areas of high unemployment.

Why has the UK government encouraged foreign multinationals?

- **J**obs – in areas of high unemployment.
- **I**nward investment – where regeneration needed after 'deindustrialisation'.
- **N**ew products – likely from some of the large innovative multinationals, with possible technology spin-offs (e.g. for the latest electronics products).
- **T**ax revenue – from profitable production in the UK.
- **O**ther multinationals may follow – e.g. from Japan or South Korea.

Several UK-based companies have subsidiaries abroad, e.g. Pilkington Glass in Australia.

MELTG!

Could you apply these to a particular case?

JINTO!

Name a Japanese company famous for its new products.

R and D and design

'Research' (not market research) means discovering new ideas for products that may be marketable (i.e. have sufficient demand) in the future.

'Development' means bringing the ideas with the greatest potential towards the market, for (hopefully) a successful launch.

But there are several pitfalls:

- **High costs** – due to expensive capital equipment and/to the time involved, e.g. for new pharmaceutical drugs.

- **Risks** – because large amounts of expenditure may be required before any return, and considerable reliance on market research data on the strength of current and future demand.

- **Cashflow problems** – caused by the initial 'net outflows' of funds [see Topic 6 Marketing, p. 60 Product life-cycle: 1 Developmnent and launch and Topic 9 Finance, p.100 Cashflow].

- **Short-termism** – e.g. if shareholders of a plc, owners expect higher dividends, rather than allowing significant investment to help the future performance of the company. Share prices will be affected.

Considered to be a problem in the UK.

'Ownership of ideas'.

'Intellectual property'

- On the one hand, governments and the Law encourage competition between businesses as it should lead to more consumer choice and lower prices [see p. 80 Competition policy].

- On the other hand, governments and the Law encourage new products, for businesses to compete internationally, and to allow the UK standard of living to rise. There are various awards, e.g. from the Design Centre and the BBC, aiming to encourage good design. The Law provides protection, from immediate competition, to individuals or businesses that come up with new ideas. By agreement within the EU, if 'intellectual property' is registered in one country, it also covers the other (14) member countries.

- The Patent Office (with its HQ relocated from London to Newport, Wales [see p. 73 Location]) is responsible for administering the four types, and providing related services, e.g. a patent search (to check if idea is new). 'Intellectual property' can be bought, sold or licensed, and can be the most valuable asset owned by a business (e.g. a famous trade mark or music).

Evaluation – the highest skill for exam answers.

(i) Patent

- Gives legal ownership of...a *new* product or process.

- Lasts for 20 years.

- E.g. a new type of television screen, widget, method of opening drink can.

(ii) Copyright

- Gives legal ownership of written documents.

- Lasts for 70 years after the death of the author (raised by the EU from the UK's traditional 50 years, in 1996).

- Automatic – no need to apply for it, but the author might have to prove it was their idea originally!

- E.g. various types of artwork, cartoons, films, music, poetry, students' essays!

(iii) Trade mark

- Gives legal ownership of a distinguishable sign (even 3D, since the Trade Mark Act 1994).

- Lasts for 10 years, but is renewable (with no maximum).

- E.g. famous brand names in clothes, perfumes, cars, a famous shaped cola bottle.

(iv) Registered design

- Gives legal ownership of outward appearance or form.

- Lasts for 5 years, but renewable (up to maximum 25 years).

- E.g. motorbike, kettle, unusual shape chocolate, fashion clothing.

- Why are companies so keen to reduce pirate copies of their goods, e.g. computer software including console games?

- Why is protecting 'intellectual property' a problem on the Internet?

> One of the types of intellectual property may be the most valuable asset the business owns → valuation problems for the Accounts?

Computer Aided Design (CAD)

CAD is now used for many products, e.g. designing and testing car components, or for designing shoes and cutting the leather with minimum waste. Set-up costs of the hardware and often customised software will be high, but considerable savings could then be possible, e.g. in terms of time saved, and less need for construction of costly prototypes or models.

> E.g. large buildings or Formula 1 cars.

Increasingly powerful hardware and complex software are allowing highly realistic testing of products on computers, even 'virtual reality'.

Costs of production

Businesses in competitive markets come under pressure to become more efficient and reduce costs.

> Always likely in an exam (including Production/O.M.).

Different types

Total Fixed Costs (TFC) = costs which will not vary with the level of output (in the short term, i.e. over a year) e.g. salaries, interest on loans, depreciation, insurance.

Total Variable Costs (TVC) = costs which will vary with the level of output (in the short term, i.e. over a year) e.g. wages, raw materials, heating, lighting, telephone/Internet.

Total Costs = TFC + TVC

$$\text{Average Fixed Costs (AFC)} = \frac{\text{TFC}}{\text{units of output}}$$

$$\text{Average Variable Costs (AVC)} = \frac{\text{TVC}}{\text{units of output}}$$

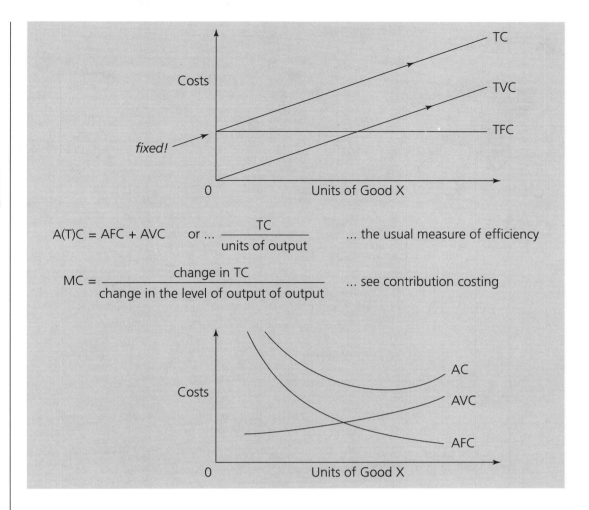

The curves are often drawn as straight lines, for simplicity (or after regression analysis!) – see p. 81 Break-even analysis.

$$A(T)C = AFC + AVC \quad \text{or} \ldots \frac{TC}{\text{units of output}} \quad \ldots \text{the usual measure of efficiency}$$

$$MC = \frac{\text{change in TC}}{\text{change in the level of output of output}} \quad \ldots \text{see contribution costing}$$

Take example data from a past exam paper or a textbook.

Costs can also be divided into:

- Direct costs – also called 'attributable costs', because they can be directly related to the production of a particular good or service, e.g. specific raw materials, just for the one product.

- Indirect costs – often called 'overheads', and not directly attributable to the particular product, e.g. salaries of directors or business rates/local taxes on the whole production site of a large diversified business, although a decision may be taken to allocate a certain percentage of them to a particular product.

Economies of scale

- Savings, i.e. reduced AC, due to the greater efficiency of larger-scale production (especially 'flow').

- The main benefits of expansion/growth of a business – organic or external.

- The *main* cause is more effective use of the fixed assets, e.g. plant and machinery [see AFC curve on diagram].

There are several different types, e.g.:

- other firms moving to the same location and sharing some costs, e.g. lighting of the industrial estate – outside the control of the business, so – **external economy**

- a larger loan having a lower rate of interest – **financial economy**

- a supertanker lowering the cost-per-litre of oil transport – **technical economy**

- a firm expanding enough to warrant a full-time accountant – **managerial economy**

In this case the whole AC curve shifts downwards.

- **The diagram:**

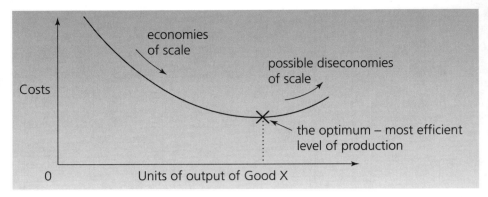

Apparently most firms do not produce at 'the optimum' ... this is only one side of the story. 'Revenue' is needed to calculate break-even and profit (or loss).

Diseconomies of scale (economic theory suggests) can arise, above a certain level of output – AC will rise, giving 'The U-shaped AC curve'. Perhaps expansion was too quick, with resultant inefficiency in storage and control of stock, or the expansion of production has created new industrial relations problems.

Types of costing

(i.e. calculating and analysing costs of production)

- **Absorption Costing** – the 'normal' type, in the sense that it includes **Total Costs (TC)**, i.e. *all* the types of costs facing the business. TC can be compared to TR (mainly from sales of the product), to check if profit, loss or break-even [see p. 81 Break-even analysis].

- **Standard Costing** – part of budgetary control, it is the estimation of likely costs of production, for comparison with the outturn – the actual costs, when known. 'variance analysis' will break down the 'adverse/negative' or 'positive variance' (i.e. difference between the two), provide reasons for the difference, and highlight inefficiencies – particularly variances in stocks of raw materials/components, labour and overheads.

- **Contribution Costing** – where a firm considers producing an order at a low price based on **Marginal Cost (MC)**. The main consideration is whether, even if an overall loss is made from the order [see Absorption costing], variable costs can be covered and a contribution made towards fixed costs.

- E.g. A business calculates that it would receive £10,000 (TR) from an order of Good X by Customer A, but TC = £12,000. However, if variable costs (TVC) happen to be £9,000, then the order might be accepted – variable costs are covered, and the order could make at least some contribution (£1,000) towards the fixed costs.

A regular in exam questions. Check on example in a past exam paper.

Reasons for accepting such a loss-making order:

- That contribution to fixed costs may be better than nothing.
- Spare capacity (including labour) will be unused otherwise.
- Keeping a valued customer for the (more profitable?) longer-term.
- Capturing a new customer, who may have further (profitable?) orders.
- Opportunity to run down surplus stocks [see p. 84 Stocks].
- Promotion of a new product.
- Promotion of a loss-leader.

But...

- Not all production can be on this basis, or an overall loss will result!
- It may store up pricing problems for the future [see Topic 6 Marketing].

Think of your own example as well.

If a teacher wanted a new phone extension in the Department, what type of costing would he/she prefer the price/charge to be based on?

Contribution costing – because the extra/marginal cost involved would be relatively low (e.g. an hour's labour, some wire, a phone).

Which type of costing would be preferred, by the farmer, for putting a new (5-mile) BT telephone line into his/her isolated farm (assuming a mobile phone is unsuitable because of signal/reception problems!)?

Absorption costing – so that the crofter is just another BT customer paying a similar charge to other customers (based on average cost).

Reducing costs

There is pressure on businesses to work within a set budget, or to become more efficient and competitive, with lower prices and/or more potential for profit (or survival).

Always likely to feature in exam questions (particularly on O.M.). Use for a piece of coursework or research assignment?

- Investing in new capital equipment with the latest technology (e.g. a faster canning plant), for economies of scale. Less energy needed.

- Deferring investment in new capital equipment! Using existing equipment will reduce budgeted costs of interest on loans, and depreciation [see Topic 9 Finance, p. 102 The balance sheet].

- Redundancies and/or natural wastage to reduce overmanning and enhance productivity. Lower wage costs over time, but extra costs initially, for administration and redundancy payments.

- 'Capping' pay increases, e.g. in line with increases in productivity, or profit-related.

- Using cheaper materials or finding suppliers with lower prices to reduce the size of working capital required, but quality might be more difficult to maintain [see p. 87, Value analysis].

- Buying stocks of raw materials or components in bulk to get 'buying economies of scale' (although possible increase in storage costs).

- Buying stocks only as required to reduce handling and storage costs [see pp. 84–87, Stocks, Just-in-Time (JIT) and 'zero stocks'].

- Introducing tighter expenditure controls and encouraging greater cost-consciousness, e.g. with advertising budgets, R and D, and heating, lighting, telephone and video-conferencing bills.

- Changing the product design, to one that is simpler and cheaper to produce, e.g. with fewer features.

- Reducing after-sales customer service/support if the Marketing Department believes this will not significantly reduce sales.

- Rationalisation, e.g. relocating or concentrating production of a particular item in one factory rather than several, to achieve economies of scale.

- Switching to a cheaper energy source, e.g. firms switching to gas in the 1990s as it became cheaper due to 'deregulation' and competition.

NB

(i) Critical Path Analysis (CPA) is commonly used on projects, to assist planning and control costs, e.g. by preventing delays [see Topic 8 Data and Information Technology, p. 94 CPA].

Paper sorting is costly, so EFT is increasingly used.

(ii) In labour-intensive production, cost-cutting will focus on reducing, or at least controlling, the wage bill, e.g. when the main High Street banks introduce new Electronic Funds Transfer (EFT) technology.

Growth of production

- **internal/organic** – mainly using reinvested/ploughed-back profits.
- **external** – mainly using integration, i.e. mergers and/or takeovers.

There are likely to be several limitations to growth:

- **Owners' objectives** – e.g. a family-owned private limited company concerned that expansion could mean 'going public' and a loss of direct control by the family.

> 'A third of businesses told researchers they wanted to remain at their existing size.'
> Survey by National Westminster Bank and The Small Business Research Trust (1/97).

- **The market** – e.g. a pub with a limited local market and little opportunity for attracting customers from further away, perhaps with a separate restaurant room.

  NB Mass production requires a very large market.

- **Availability of capital** – e.g. banks being cautious in the 1990s, after experiences in late 1980s, when they expanded lending during 'the Lawson Boom' but then had to write off record levels of bad debts, as many businesses had financial problems in the following recession [see Topic 10 External influences].

- **Management techniques/skills** – e.g. the directors of a manufacturing company not realising (or not until it is too late) that significant expansion can mean changes to the chain of command, span of control, and techniques which existing management may not have [e.g. see Topic 2 Objectives, p. 8 MBO and Topic 4 Management and leadership].

> 'Smaller businesses with potential for development into larger-scale enterprises face three substantial barriers to their growth: lack of strategic skills among managers, an inadequate supply of external risk capital, and limited government encouragement for the businesses to develop and expand.
>
> Smaller businesses of 50 to 500 employees play a vital role in translating new scientific and technological knowledge into economic wealth. They also provide the pool of companies from which some of the leading international businesses of the future are expected to emerge.'
> The Enterprise Challenge: overcoming barriers to growth in small firms, report by Advisory Council for Science and Technology (7/90).

- **Human resource factors** – e.g. workers relocated to a new site of an expanding company, with a less-motivating working environment and atmosphere. Were they willing to move? Were they consulted over the move? [see Topic 5 Human resource management, p. 34 Change].

- **Diseconomies of scale** – e.g. a business expanding too quickly and the warehousing sysytem not being geared up to handle and/or store extra stock [see p. 84 Stocks], or industrial relations problems being created – either type of problem could raise costs rather than permitting the desired increased economies of scale.

- **Competition policy** – e.g. the Office of Fair Trading (OFT) referring a possible merger between two large brewing companies to the Monopolies and Mergers Commission (MMC), because the new business will have substantial monopoly power within the market, leading to higher prices and/or less choice.

In spite of possible 'economies of scale'.

It tries for a balance between protecting consumers and not discouraging large UK businesses, e.g. in banking and telecommunications. There seems to be less conflict, than initially thought, over the objectives of the UK and the EU policies.

Three other key aspects of analysing costs

(a) Opportunity cost

Refers to the sacrificed alternatives involved in a decision on the use of resources, e.g. a government increasing expenditure on one project and sacrificing expenditure on another. Or a business deciding to invest a substantial amount in a new computer intranet instead of increasing expenditure on something else. [See p. 93 Decision trees.]

Individuals continually face such decisions, e.g. whether to do X or Y.

(b) Cost-benefit analysis (CBA)

Regularly used from the mid-1960s on, CBA is often used as an essential planning tool for new projects, taking into account wider aspects than just private [fixed and variable] costs, e.g. for a nuclear power station, the Humber Bridge, the Channel Tunnel, a new motorway, or building and operating a new petfood factory in a small market town:

Strictly speaking the 'social costs' will include the 'private costs'.

Private costs	Revenue
• fixed, e.g. interest on a loan • variable, e.g. stocks of raw materials	• sales of the product

Social (or external) costs	Social benefits
• pollution – factory noise and smell • pollution – lorry transport • traffic and accidents increase • effects on local wildlife and tourism	• employment – new jobs • boost to local economy – people's incomes • boost to local economy – local businesses • sponsorship of local sports clubs

But...

- Full analysis can be complex, time-consuming and expensive.

- Difficult to give a precise financial measure to each cost (e.g. increased accident risks) or benefit (e.g. commuter time saved using a bridge). Critics have claimed it 'attempts to measure the unmeasurable'.

- The final decision may still not be clear-cut, e.g. one benefit outweighing several costs, or vice versa, and may still require a political verdict.

Four aspects to be understood.

(c) Break-even analysis

(i) Definition A business will break even where total revenue from sales of the product (and possibly assets, e.g. land) just covers total operating costs:

- TR > TC ...profit
- TR < TC ...loss
- TR = TC ...break-even

Only three possibilities!

(ii) Diagram: Hopefully, the TR and TC curves/lines will cross:

So the break-even level of output could change, if there is a change in:

- TR, e.g. change in price and/or number of the product sold and/or...
- TC, e.g. a rise in interest rates would push up the (fixed) costs of borrowing, or a fall in the price of a main raw material would reduce (variable) costs.

- The margin of safety is the difference between a particular (e.g. current) level of production and the break-even level. A rise in interest rates would reduce the margin of safety.

(iii) Formula: Besides checking where TR = TC on a graph or in a table [see below], it may be easier (with the data given) to use the formula:

$$\text{Break-Even Quantity (BEQ)} = \frac{\text{TFC}}{\text{unit price/AR} - \text{AVC}}$$

e.g. Calculate the BEQ for 'Small Boardgames Ltd', which has fixed costs of £30,000, variable costs per product of £3, and sells a game for £8:

$$\text{BEQ} = \frac{30,000}{8 - 3} = 6,000 \text{ boardgames}$$

(iv) A case study:

Costs of production at the Acme Springwater Co. Ltd are:

Output (bottles per week)	TC £'s per wk.	TR £'s per wk.
0	5,000	
10,000	8,000	
20,000	13,000	
30,000	17,000	
40,000	20,000	
50,000	24,000	
60,000	29,500	

The small bottles of the springwater are sold to pubs, hotels and restaurants at 50p each without any discounts for bulk-buying.

- Put in the TR data, i.e. 0 x 50p = £0, 20,000 x 50p = £10,000 etc. At what level does TR = TC? [40,000 bottles per week?]

- What is the most profitable level of output, i.e. the maximum TR – TC? [At output 50,000 bottles, TR = £25,000 and TC = £24,000, i.e. £1,000 per week.]

*Advantages of using **break-even analysis:***

- relatively straightforward

- relatively cheap

- shows the relationship between the types of costs

- could highlight problems for management to tackle.

Disadvantages:

- time and costs of collecting data

- reliability of the data – is it up-to-date?

- to some extent 'forecasts are always wrong'

- the assumption that all the products will be sold and bring in TR (i.e. not produced for stock).

Work study

- A management tool to improve productivity of humans and equipment.

- Attempts to use objective **methods** to measure and suggest improvements, e.g. to avoid bottlenecks in a production line.

- Pioneered by F. W. Taylor [see Topic 5 Human resource management, p. 22 Motivation] as part of 'scientific management' (in early 1900s).

- Concentration on the short-term (so not for long-term investment projects).

- Just one technique to use (so not a panacea for production problems).

- Often carried out by external management consultants/specialists.

- A mixed reputation – workers seeing benefits to resulting improvements (e.g. better piece-rate pay), or resenting managers checking up on them.

There are two types:

- **Method study** – a detailed analysis of how a task is performed, making the improvements, and monitoring performance regularly.

- **Time study or work measurement** – a detailed analysis of speed of performance, allowing for individuals' need and fatigue, to establish a defined standard time for a task.

Possible benefits include:

- increased productivity, with savings of effort and time

- reducing health and safety risks

- reduced errors and wastage caused by inefficient working practices

- encouraging planned maintenance, including cost benefits from regular preventative maintenance, e.g. by a coach firm

Give an example each of an objective and a subjective statement.

Henry Ford was impressed!

- increased job satisfaction felt by the worker
- helping managers devise effective training schemes.

> 'It will be the system, not the people, which is at fault if efficiency and quality is lost.'
> Dr W. E. Deming (1954).

Activity sampling involves taking a large number of random 'snapshots' of a type of work, e.g. a manager performing a certain number of tasks in an ad hoc manner, where a specific work study may not be appropriate. A pattern may emerge, which can be used to define the work, and then attempts can be made to improve overall productivity.

Ergonomics is the study of humans in the working environment, with the application of anatomical, physiological and psychological knowledge. Unlike work study, it starts with human behaviour (rather than a task) and analyses how workplaces could be designed better around the capabilities of the operator. Economic, technological and social pressures have forced businesses to adapt some jobs to suit employees.

Apparently increasingly important – so more likely to feature in exam questions.

The working environment

In other words the site, the local work area, and the equipment to be used.

It is a crucial determinant of the productivity of the humans and thus the overall efficiency of production. The workplace is one of the 'hygiene factors' analysed by Frederick Herzberg [see Topic 5 Human resource management, p. 22 Motivation].

EU Workplace (Health, Safety and Welfare) Regulations 1992 tidied up several previous laws and set general requirements [see Topic 5 Human resource management, p. 48 The Law] e.g. on the working environment:

- temperature in indoor workplaces
- ventilation
- lighting, including emergency lighting
- room dimensions and space
- suitability of workstations and seating.

Stocks

Identify the stocks needed for the exam case study, or particular question.

Businesses will need stocks (or inventories), which are recorded as current assets (i.e. ready for use) in the Accounts – if they change in value there will be 'stock appreciation' or a 'stock depreciation' [see Topic 9 Finance, p. 105 Depreciation]. There are three types:

- **Raw materials** – including components and consumables, to allow continuous production.
- **Work-in-progress** – goods and services at an intermediate/part-complete stage of production, and goods in transit to customers.
- **Finished goods** – i.e. goods ready for distribution to customers [see Topic 6 Marketing, p. 64 Channel of distribution].

What type of business could have 'zero work-in-progress'?

Holding stocks

Stocks can be expensive and they tie up working capital which could otherwise be reduced or used in another way [see Topic 9 Finance, p. 100 Working capital].

But...

- Demand may be difficult to predict (e.g. in fashion items) and lack of stocks of finished products may lose sales to the competition or damage a reputation for reliable customer service. 'Buffer stocks' [see diagram] may be built up ready to be run down during peak-time demand (e.g. for ice cream in a heatwave).

- Supply capacity may not match peak-time demand (e.g. for Easter eggs or Christmas crackers), so stocks are built up off-season.

- Long production cycles (e.g. of timber and malt whisky which need to mature) will incur large stocks of work-in-progress, as will long-distance transport.

- Decoupling processes will mean that one production process does not have to wait for another to be finished (e.g. kit-car production waiting for engines).

- Economies of scale may result from flow production and ordering raw materials or components in larger bulk. A comparison would be made between extra handling and storage costs, and savings by buying and transporting in larger bulk.

Control of stocks

Opportunity cost decisions have to be made on the level of stocks.

Just-in-Case (JIC)

See JIC below.

- 'Buffer stocks' of raw materials or components are held to prevent disruption of production if they ran out.

- Stocks of finished products are held to cope with fluctuations in demand and avoid the risk of 'stock out' – customers may switch to a rival product.

- Used particularly in main Western economies until the 1990s.

Do you know of a case where a shop was out of stock of an item?

JIC – notice the differences with JIT.

Just-in-Time (JIT)

- Part of **lean production**, to minimise costs of holding and handling stocks.

- Stocks of raw materials or components arrive just before required.

- No work-in-progress costs (including storage), but revenue delayed.

- Stocks of finished products shipped out as soon as possible, sometimes within hours.

- No buffer stocks needed.

- 'Lead or procurement time' and reorder quantity reduced.

- Pioneered in the 1970s by Toyota, and labelled **kanban**.

Not a lot of people know this!

- The kanban is a computerised tag permitting the next stage of production, and its use enables strict control over stocks.

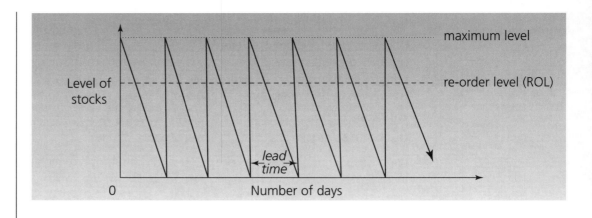

'In the UK, car manufacturer Nissan has electronic links to suppliers of radiators, seats and other components, which enables it to send orders just 45 minutes before the items are needed on the production line.'

The Times (29/1/97).

No buffer / safety stocks.

JIT involves:

- production being continually market-led
- raw materials delivered only as required (daily?), to the point of use
- work-in-progress only moving to a next stage as needed
- finished goods only being produced to order, i.e. if sold
- close co-operation between manufacturer and suppliers
- a flexible and reliable production line, including the workforce
- the slowest process governs overall speed of production.

Can you draw and label the JIC and JIT diagrams, without looking them up – ready for an exam answer?

Some businesses now aim for 'zero stocks':

- raw materials only delivered/taken as required [see Topic 9 Finance, p. 100 Cashflow]
- zero work-in-progress, with all products ready for the customer
- finished products not stored, but in transit to the customers within hours.

There are inherent risks with JIT but the significant cost savings, in competitive markets, have made it attractive to UK businesses. Guaranteed deliveries of raw materials or components, at the right time and in the right place, become even more of a priority than the price.

ABC analysis

This is used to identify the more expensive stocks to hold, and which therefore require more careful monitoring (perhaps including a Work Study). The analysis is also known as 'Pareto Analysis' after the economist Alfredo Pareto whose research suggested that 20% of items will account for 80% of TC – 'The 80-20 Law'.

You are unlikely to have to make calculations in an exam.

Stocks are divided into three categories, according to 'Annual Usage Value':

AUV = price per item/unit x annual usage

'Class A' stocks have a relatively high AUV, so require careful monitoring with frequent and relatively small orders.

'Class B' stocks are on ROL basis. Order quantities are reviewed fairly frequently.

'Class C' stocks receive less frequent and stringent controls.

Economic order quantity (EOQ)

This is a formula to determine the optimum quantity, balancing costs of ordering stocks with costs of holding more stocks.

$$EOQ = 2 S D/I$$

S = ordering costs (per order)

D = total annual number of units demanded

I = cost of holding 1 unit for a year

Number of orders placed will therefore be D/EOQ, with the (computerised) formula being adjusted to allow for bulk discounts and warehousing space.

Value analysis

Another (American) label is 'value management'!

More recently re-labelled 'value engineering', this involves a team deciding on a compromise between satisfying the customer and controlling costs, e.g. a team set up to decide on the launch of a new fruit drink might include:

- Brand manager – with special responsibility for marketing the product.
- Designer (free-lance or in-house) – for ideas on the new can design.
- Production manager – responsible for any necessary changes to production.
- Buyer of fruit concentrate – to confirm supply contracts, and likely price trends.
- An accountant – to decide on type of costing and to consider the various costs.

A VA team will seek to achieve a balance between:

- Function – does the product perform well, e.g. quench thirst?
- Aesthetics – is the product attractive in appearance?
- Economics – can it be produced cost-effectively?

NB Possible conflict between one or more of these, e.g. expensive packaging needed for an aesthetically-pleasing product, so a compromise between the three 'pulls' might have to be worked on during the R and D stages.

Quality

In business, quality does not necessarily mean excellence, e.g. a cheap ball-point pen could be 'a quality product', so...

> *'Quality is meeting or exceeding customers' expectation at a price that represents value to them.'*
> H. J. Harrington of IBM, *The Improvement Process* (1987).

> *'Quality is delighting the customer by continuously meeting and improving upon agreed requirements.'*
> Macdonald and Piggott, *Global Quality: the new management culture* (1990).

The 'kitemark'.

In 1979 the British Standards Institute (BSI) introduced the world's first published quality standard. BS5750 was a method of writing and establishing the best working practices, and could apply to management methods and/or work instructions. Doctors' surgeries, advertising agencies, multinationals, or any other type of organisation could apply to be registered and, if awarded the standard, use the BSI's 'Registered Firm' logo on signs and documents.

Increasingly competitive markets in the 1990s meant even more emphasis on quality, with 20,000 firms registering for BS5750 by 1993.

The Department of Trade and Industry (DTI) introduced its 'Getting to grips with quality' campaign...

Ensuring quality

Inspection of the final product is one method of quality control, but carries high rectification costs because by then it is usually too late. VW's Wolfsburg factory in Germany still had problems in the mid-1990s with faults on Golfs coming off production lines. In the average time it took VW to rectify the faults on a car, Toyota could build another vehicle!

> 'Cease dependence on mass inspection: build quality into the product in the first place.'
> Dr W. Edwards Deming (1954!)

Quality control means concern for maintaining set standards throughout manufacturing or tertiary production process. Dr Deming [see Topic 5 Human resource management, p. 22 Motivation] encouraged Japanese businesses, in their rebuilding after World War II, to develop techniques in order to be competitive in world markets.

> 'Profit in business comes from repeat customers, customers that boast about your product and service, and that bring friends with them.'
> Dr W. Edwards Deming

(a) **Total quality management (TQM)** was adopted in Japan and, since the mid-1980s, by many American and European businesses. All employees are involved in achieving 'quality' – standards are laid down, and communicated to all employees, who receive appropriate training. Initial high costs are outweighed by greater longer-term benefits of enhanced reputation and competitiveness, as well as cost savings due to reduced errors/wastage.

(b) **Kaizen** is a programme designed to improve productivity and quality, by small but continuous increments, i.e. not by few, but large, step changes. The (apparently unattainable) target is 'zero defects', achieved by eliminating 'three deadly sins':

   • *muda* – 'waste' in Japanese

   • *mura* – inconsistent use of a machine or employee

   • *muri* – imposition of excessive demands on machines or workers.

> '3 things are necessary for kaizen to be successful...Senior management commitment, senior management commitment, and senior management commitment.'
> Director of the Kaizen Institute, Tokyo (1995).

Point made!

(c) **Quality circles** consist of small groups of workers (4–12) from the same work area [see Topic 5 Human resource management, p. 19 Groups], who agree to meet regularly to identify, investigate and resolve production problems. The idea started in Japan (in 1962), with an estimated one million by 1980. By 1985 there were only 400-500 in UK manufacturing, and 40-50 in UK services.

Benefits claimed for quality circles include:

- improved communications
- more harmonious work environment
- more involvement and commitment
- personal skill and social development
- personal growth
- effective use of capital and human resources
- greater job flexibility
- increased productivity
- greater safety awareness
- higher levels of quality
- lower costs
- less conflict.

Why the delay in their introduction to the UK?

Quality circles only seem to work (e.g with Rover's 'associates') when there is clear senior management commitment! In an autocratic work environment members of a quality circle can become frustrated when their suggestions are ignored by the management.

Quality assurance

This is where a supplier guarantees the quality of goods, and even encourages representatives of the customers to visit the production lines regularly. The supplier benefits from knowing the customers' exact requirements/ specifications, reducing the number of rejects (which involve costs and perhaps lost customers), and gaining continuous feedback.

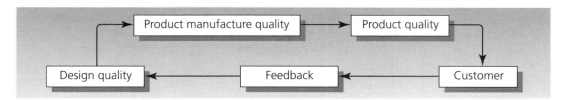

The customer benefits from cost savings resulting from fewer 'goods inward' inspections being necessary, leading to more harmonious business relations.

> 'Nissan says that when it first set up in the UK in the mid-1980s it used to reject 2,000 parts per million from its first 200 supplying firms. Now its rejection rate from its top 50 suppliers is down to 10 parts per million – equal to the best rates in Japan.'
>
> The Times (19/11/96).

ISO9000

This International Standards Organisation, applicable in the EU's Single Market, replaced BS5750 as the main quality standard in 1994, but the aims remained the same.

> ...'to encourage the provision of a good or service that consistently meets the needs of the customer within a management framework that encourages a process of continuous improvement'.
>
> BSI Journal (12/94).

But some critics have said:

- more a guarantee of consistency rather than high quality
- a marketing tool rather than an emphasis on continually enhancing production
- assessors for the standard are 'not properly monitored', and complaints have come from businesses (including some awarded the standard) of assessment carried out subjectively.

Benchmarking

Best Practice Benchmarking (BPB) is a method of discovering ways to improve production standards, perhaps as part of a kaizen philosophy (i.e. making continual improvement). As with 'benchmarking' of computer hardware and software (e.g. for speed of operation), comparisons can be made. The desired standard may be a notch up from that achieved previously within the firm, or one achieved by most businesses in the industry.

The standard could relate to the amount of R and D (p. 75), Lead time (p. 85), or ROCE [see Topic 9 Finance, p. 103 Ratios], as well as reliability or some other aspect of quality.

Information could be gained from specialist newspaper and magazine articles, market reports, specialist firms (and their databases of relevant information), or by asking suppliers and customers.

Sometimes industrial espionage is used – but what about the legal and ethical aspects?

Capacity utilisation

This is the extent to which a business is using all the available resources, particularly its main fixed assets, i.e. the buildings and capital equipment. Are they being fully used, or could AFC [see Topic 7 Operations management, p. 76 Costs] be brought down further?

$$\text{Capacity utilisation } \% = \frac{\text{current output per week}}{\text{potential output per week}} \times 100$$

Data and information technology

Examples – from a case study?

Quantitative data – in the form of numbers, e.g. numerical and statistical results of experiments, results of questionnaires (if choices were made from a fixed range of answers), surveys (e.g. a production process), data in rank order (e.g. on product quality), demographic data, or financial data (e.g. on a Balance Sheet).

Qualitative data – in words or illustrations, without numbers, e.g. descriptive results of experiments, quotations from questionnaires or interviews, observations of people's or businesses' actions, or data from maps, photos, marketing materials, or company reports.

Primary data – collected with a specific purpose in mind, e.g. a 'census' (asking every member of the population) or 'sampling' (a targeted group of the population).

Secondary data – for another purpose besides the original reason, e.g. 'internal' (from within the company, e.g. stock lists, costings, or employee details), or 'external' (e.g. from the government, newspapers, CBI, TUC, or OECD).

Methodology

Marks are often awarded in coursework for explaining these aspects.

- Why those particular methods used, e.g. interviews, or questionnaires, or 'desk research'? Which type of each – e.g. an informal semi-structured interview?

- How was data recorded? Was it done accurately?

- Confidentiality a problem – in collection or reporting of data?

- Bias reduced to a minimum, or even eliminated? E.g. when a researcher is subjective about an organisation they know well, or when designing a questionnaire to receive objective answers.

Sampling

Who will be in 'the target population'? A sample needs to be representative and while large samples give greater accuracy, they are more expensive (e.g. a full national census costs £ millions, every decade). The following methods are used:

- **Random sampling** – every member of the target group/population has an equal chance of being chosen (by computer?). Selection is unbiased.

- **Stratified sampling** – used where there are distinguishable subgroups in the overall group, e.g. different socio-economic groups. Members of each subgroup may then be chosen randomly, avoiding selective bias.

- **Cluster sampling** – when a geographical area is selected, then *all* of the members of that local group/population are sampled, e.g. a survey of small retailers.

- **Quota sampling** – commonly used in market research, because relatively cheap and convenient. Smaller groups/quotas can be chosen if the researcher has details of the total population and can thus ensure they are representative.

- **Systematic sampling** means, for example, selecting every tenth item or person on a list of the total group (which strictly speaking should be randomly compiled, i.e. not alphabetically).

Use for your own piece of research/ coursework?

- **Convenience/opportunity sampling** may be the best compromise for a piece of small-scale research, when time, finance and ability to travel are limited. The sample may have to be restricted to the one that can be reached conveniently. Acknowledgement of, and allowance for, the limitations is advisable (and gets marks in a research assignment!).

Presenting quantitative data

Good communication requires clear, relevant and unambiguous data.

- **Tabulation** – using labelled rows and columns, with units and the source given.
- **Graphs** – line diagrams which plot a series of values as points joined by straight lines, particularly useful for comparisons of trends. A title, labelled axes, and the source, are important.
- Diagrams:
  - **Bar charts** – quantitative data is displayed in horizontal or vertical bars, with the aim of a quick visual impact. Width of bars should be uniform, and they should not touch unless a comparison is made within a category.
  - **Histograms** – similar to bar charts, but width of the bars is important, and they should also be touching.
  - **Pictograms** – similar to bar charts but bars are represented pictorially, for further visual impact. Pictures might make precise comparisons difficult, or even misleading, unless numbers are added alongside.
  - **Pie charts** – circles representing the total data, with sectors/'slices' drawn in proportion to represent relative importance or frequency of each component.

> ### Averages
>
> **The mean** – most commonly used average, calculated by dividing the total by the number of component parts.
>
> **The mode** – the most frequently occurring item.
>
> **The median** – the middle item in a series.

Index numbers

An index is a single figure summing up a complicated set of figures, and starts at 100 in the 'base year' (e.g. 1995 = 100). Once the composition of the index is understood, the number of points increase or decrease will show the trend, whether the index is regularly taken back to 100 (e.g. to measure changes in the sterling trade-weighted/'basket-of-currencies' index), or allowed to go on into the 000s.

- **FTSE 100 Index** ('The Footsie') – consists of share price movements of the 100 largest plcs (by capitalisation), to represent a daily barometer of the health of UK businesses, or at least what the market thinks of them at that time. (The FT Index only includes 30 plcs, so is quoted less often.)
- 'In real terms' or 'at 199? prices' – data adjusted to allow for inflation.
- 'Current prices' – data not adjusted for inflation.
- **Index of retail prices (RPI)** or Cost of living index – the usual measure of inflation, using a representative sample of households' purchases which are weighted according to how much is spent on each type of good or service. According to the movements of the Index, the inflation rate will be quoted as an annual % rate [see Topic 10 External influences, p. 121].

Newspapers try to vary the methods of presentation – can you find examples?

When is each of these used?

Shares – daily (even hourly) economic measures are rare.

Inflation – seen as 'Public enemy no. 1' since the mid-1970s.

Using the RPI, another index can allow for inflation/the changing value of money, to make comparison of data easier, e.g. for 'Gross National Product' – total output of goods and services of the domestic economy ('GDP') plus the balance of currency flows from UK businesses abroad (minus currency flowing from the economy to foreign businesses). Dividing by the size of population, gives GNP per capita – usual measure of the standard of living [see Topic 2 Objectives, p. 7 Governments].

Decision trees

- A representation of the possible outcomes of a decision.
- An aid to management decision-making.
- The most profitable outcome can be identified.
- Drawn from left to right.
- Small squares = decision nodes/stages.
- Small circles = outcome nodes.
- 0.8, 0.2, etc. represent probability of the outcome.
- The final decision can be based on all the data.

E.g. Invest £100,000 in a new computer system, or in launching a new product, or neither. Estimates suggests that if the new computer system fulfils its potential it could boost sales by £200,000 a year, if not then £80,000 is likely. Market research suggests that the new product could bring in an extra £300,000 if successful, or £120,000 if not.

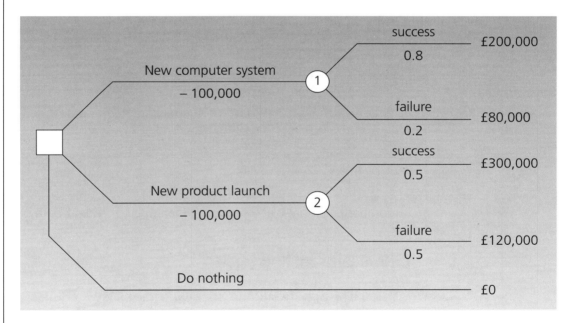

Advantages:
- all possible outcomes are considered (including doing nothing)
- risk is considered as a key factor
- more objective discussion, e.g. based on quantitative market research.

Disadvantages:
- accuracy depends on data used
- quantifying precise probabilities
- oversimplification of the decisions involved
- management bias could still be present.

Time series

Again, the idea is not complex.

The analysis can identify trends in data for a business or an economy.

- Moving totals – for identifying a long-term trend...

e.g. a three-month moving total for sales of a local newspaper – what is the trend?

Month	Sales	3-month m.t.
Jan.	21,000	
Feb.	24,000	
Mar.	17,000	62,000
April	21,000	62,000
May	27,000	65,000
June	25,000	73,000

The three-month moving total (m.t.) is the sum of the current and previous two months' totals.

- Moving averages – for revealing underlying trends....

e.g. a three-month moving average for a local train service – what is the trend?

Show your working in an exam question.

Month	Ticket sales	3-month centred m.a.
Jan.	110,000	
Feb.	145,000	130,000
Mar.	135,000	133,333
April	140,000	145,000
May	160,000	180,000
June	240,000	200,000
July	200,000	

...three-month m.a. is centred on the middle month, e.g.
May = (140,000+160,000+240,000) divided by three.

A six-month m.a., for example, would be the average of the two relevant three-month centred m.a.s.

- Seasonally adjusted means data adjusted to get to the underlying trend, e.g. the number of school-leavers in July affecting employment data.

Critical path analysis (CPA)

CPA is a type of Network Analysis, defined by BS4335 as ' a group of techniques for presenting information to assist project planning and control'.

Again, the underlying objective is straight-forward.

Activities – part of a project, shown by an arrow from left to right and with an identifying letter and the time (hours, weeks or months) it is estimated to take. Some activities cannot be started until others are completed.

Nodes – where activities start and end, shown by a circle.

Each one is numbered (in the left-hand semi-circle), and has an 'earliest start time' (EST) and 'latest finish time' (LFT).

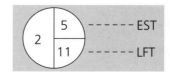

E.g. in a project involving five tasks/activities, activity B has to wait until A is finished, C has to wait until A and B are over, and E has to wait until all the others are completed...

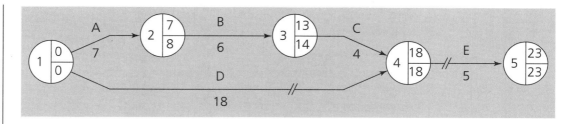

- Each EST adds in the time taken for the previous activity. At node 4 the EST has to be based on the longer of the two previous-activity times (i.e. 18 from activity D).
- Critical activities (i.e. the ones that must be completed on time if the whole project is not to be delayed) are on the longest way round – the critical path (marked by two small dashes across each activity line/arrow).
- LFTs are worked out from end/right to start/left, subtracting activity times along the critical path.
- Nodes for critical activities have EST = LFT , i.e. no 'float time'.
- Float time – spare time for each activity before a delay would result.
  - (a) **Free float**, i.e. before the next activity would be delayed
    = EST of the next activity minus duration of this activity minus EST of this activity.
  - (b) **Total float**, i.e. if the whole project is not to be delayed
    = LFT of this activity minus duration of this activity minus EST of this activity.

Advantages:
- precise planning encouraged, which should help the execution of the project
- time saved by identifying which tasks can be carried out at the same time
- stocks could be ordered (JIT [see Topic 7 Operations management, p. 85] according to the forecast EST helping the cashflow [see Topic 9 Finance, p. 100] of the business
- problems, e.g. if a delay does occur, may be easier to tackle using the analysis.

Disadvantages:
- activity arrows are not drawn to (time) scale
- complex analysis may be needed on large projects, although computers can help
- time schedules will still need to be adhered to, if a project is to be effectively managed.

Using information technology

Information processing:
- personal computer (PC)/terminal
- word processor
- computer memory storage/databases
- manipulation of data, e.g. spreadsheets
- software to aid decision-making
- software for CAD
- software to produce graphics, forms, mailings etc.

Information transmission:
- 'intranets' – internal networks
- mobile telecommunications, e.g. phones
- the Internet
- E-mail
- faxes by telephone lines

Try at least one each of these. Get the right one for the particular question. Show your working.

For evaluation.

Identify examples for each of these.

- teletext, e.g. for exchange rates
- electronic funds transfer (EFT)
- teleconferencing
- electronic data exchange, i.e. computer to computer.

Evaluation. Can you apply these to a particular case study?

Advantages of using IT:
- reductions in costs – in data storage and retrieval, on overheads and labour
- quality – word processing may improve documentation
- information – can be more easily stored, retrieved, processed and accessed
- complex numerical information – more easily manipulated and conveyed
- CAD – facilitates design functions, and usually faster [see Topic 7 Operations management]
- security – computer-held data may be more secure than that in filing cabinets
- presentations – e.g. for sales or training, can be easier and of better quality.

You need to know more how businesses use IT, rather than having to use it yourself.

Disadvantages:
- increased costs – initially, and if manual backup still needed
- quality – might reduce if human skills lost
- loss of data – if computer crashes, with no backup
- security – if outsiders can gain information, for industrial espionage or fraud, e.g. syphoning off funds, or deleting data with a virus.

In every organisation there will be an individual, or a department, responsible for managing the financial aspects. There will be a need to:

- assess potential uses of the financial resources

- acquire financial resources from suitable sources

- manage the resources according to budgets

- account for how the resources were used.

Management accounting – the provision of financial information for particular questions, to help managers solve specific problems.

Financial accounting – Small businesses, including most sole traders, partnerships and some private limited companies, simply have to publish details of their finances for tax purposes. Self-assessment of the tax liability is now required. The owners will receive details of the Accounts.

What is the difference between 'Ltd' and 'plc'?

Public limited companies (plcs) have to lodge a copy of 'The Annual Accounts' with the Registrar of Companies. Shareholders must receive copies, along with 'The Report to Shareholders' from the Board of Directors. This 'financial accounting' provides information to several stakeholders interested in the performance of the particular business. The Accounts have to be checked by independent auditors, called chartered accountants, paid for by the company, who may sign a report to confirm the Accounts 'represent a true and fair view' of a company's performance and situation.

In the 1960s accountants came under pressure to standardise accounting procedures and results, to improve consistency, quality and usefulness of financial data, but the first 'Statement of Standard Accounting Practice (SSAP)' was introduced in 1970. Companies Acts 1985 and 1989 specified in detail how companies must construct balance sheets and profit and loss accounts. By the 1990s there were 23 SSAPs. In 1990 the Accounting Standards Board was set up, and SSAPs were now called 'Financial Reporting Standards (FRS)'.

> 'The number of directors banned or disqualified increased nearly 50% last year, according to the Department of Trade and Industry (DTI)...The rise is partly because of new reporting standards introduced last September, which make it easier for insolvency practitioners to identify and report misconduct. Ministers are keen to promote a healthy business climate in which enterprise can flourish.'
>
> The Times (5/6/97).

In an ever-changing business world, agreed accounting concepts, i.e. underlying/basic ideas and conventions, i.e. the usual methods used) have been important.

Accounting concepts

- **Going concern** – accounts are prepared on the understanding that the business will continue to operate in the foreseeable future. Assets are valued according to historic cost, rather than the realisable value (i.e. the value if sold) which would be more important if the business were planning to close down.

- **Consistency** – the same methods of calculating and presenting information, e.g. for depreciation, for comparisons and noting trends.

- **Accruals** – costs and types of revenue are matched to the time of use (by the company) or purchase (by the customer), *not* when payment was made or received.
- **Prudence** – perhaps to balance over-optimism of other managers, accountants need to be conservative, e.g. valuing assets at the lower end of the range, being pessimistic on future tax bills, and regarding invoices (not quotations) as 'sales'.

Accounting conventions

The usual accepted methods.

- **Objectivity** – using measurable and independently verifiable information.
- **Separate entity** – the company is recognised in law in its own right.
- **Money measurement** – all assets and liabilities recorded in the same units of currency, except for goodwill and management skills which, although potentially very valuable, may be considered unmeasurable in money terms.
- **Historic cost** – all items initially valued at cost, and then depreciation can be subtracted, or appreciation added, (e.g. for land rising in value).
- **Double-entry book-keeping** (even on computer!) – every transaction of the business being recorded in two ways: 'giving' and 'receiving', as a check.

Sources of finance

Longer-term 'capital' is needed for setting up (or buying) a business, and growth, which can be either 'organic' or 'external' [see Topic 7 Operations management, p. 80 Limitations to growth].

Short-term 'working capital' is needed for running a business from month to month [see p. 100 Cashflow].

Which sources are available to each business? [see Topic 1 Types of businesses]. Which are most commonly used?...

Do you need to check up on any of these?

(Usually) longer-term	Short-term
• owner's capital	• borrowing from friends or relatives
• savings/reserves	• bank overdraft (or short-term loan)
• reinvested profits/ploughing back	• trade credit
• selling/liquidating assets	• factoring
• bank loan/mortgage	
• hire purchase (HP)	
• redundancy payment (lump sum)	
• sleeping partner	
• sale and leaseback	
• share and 'debenture' issues	
• venture capital	
• government grants or subsidies – when available?	

The 'long-term' can vary from industry to industry.

Choosing the source

Evaluation.

- **Time and objectives**

  Short-termism might be a problem, with shareholders of a limited company expecting high dividends rather than allowing profits to remain undistributed and ploughed back into the business. Time would also be important regarding when any borrowing has to be repaid – an *in*flow of funds will be needed at that time.

- ### Amount needed

  Banks use computer formulae to calculate the maximum loan that would available to a particular individual or business, and other sources will also have a limit, depending on the situation at the time. For a limited company, issuing shares is itself costly, so only suitable for larger amounts of (long-term) finance.

- ### Purpose

  Risks may put off some potential sources, and owners rather than lenders will be expected to contribute the main part of the finance. It is more difficult to raise capital for new ventures and for certain products [see p. 104 ROCE].

- ### Reputation and creditworthiness

  A good business reputation, especially if it includes well-known brands, will make it easier to raise funds. Having no problems with previous use of a particular source of finance will also help.

- ### Economic environment

  Events in the market, e.g. a change in fashion, or in the economy, e.g. a change in interest rates, can affect the expected return on the venture, and make a source of finance more or less attractive, and/or available, to a business.

How much borrowing?

A crucial 'opportunity cost' decision.

How much finance a business raises depends on its size and its objectives, e.g. survival (in a recession) or expansion (in an economic boom). A limited company seeking to grow 'organically' or 'externally' may have the choice of raising capital by issuing shares/equity or borrowing/debt.

Gearing measures the borrowing of a business compared to the total amount of finance put into the business:

$$\text{Gearing ratio} = \frac{\text{long-term liabilities or debts}}{\text{capital employed}}$$

There are various forms of this ratio, but all are based on the same principle.

In 1966, Laker Airways started Skytrain services, offering cheaper tickets on transatlantic flights. The service proved popular and the business expanded rapidly. The public were surprised when, in 1982, the airline went into liquidation – once the main assets, the aircraft, had been sold off, there was no hope of a relaunch. A main problem was shown in the Accounts – the airline's borrowing had increased from £37 million in 1979 to £111 million in 1980! The growth had been rapid, with apparently healthy profits, but borrowing went too far – the airline had become too 'highly-geared'. (In 1996 Sir Freddie Laker's new airline began its first flights.)

Creditors have a prior claim on the year's profits, so dividends on shares are more liable to fluctuations if a firm is highly-geared, (i.e. with large interest payments), which often deters cautious investors (e.g. large pension funds and insurance companies), but speculative investors may be attracted if substantial profits cover the debts, and there are relatively high dividends and good prospects for the future are evident.

Debt/borrowing:
- pay interest
- repay capital
- interest tax-deductible
- a set period.

Equity/shares:
- do not *have* to pay dividends
- rarely repay capital
- dividends *not* tax-deductible
- a long-term commitment.

Working capital is the amount of short-term finance needed by a business, e.g. to cover the costs of wages, raw materials, work-in-progress, and consumables. Interest will have to be paid if this finance is raised through credit/borrowing, e.g. through a regular bank overdraft.

> *'Working capital is the amount of finance needed to power the business – it is like the fuel tank on a car. Of course greater fuel economy will help the business.'*
>
> 'Easy Money', BBC video series for small businesses (10/94).

There are two important elements:

- what the business is owed by debtors
- what the business owes to creditors, e.g. for supplies of raw materials.

Overtrading, where invoices/bills to be paid by the business are not being covered sufficiently quickly by sales revenue from customers paying on their invoices, can face a business expanding quickly. Increases in stocks and in amounts owed by debtors will lead to more working capital being required.

However, there could be a considerable reduction in costs if the size of the working capital could be reduced.

- Reduce the costs of current assets [see p. 102 The balance sheet] e.g. shop around for cheaper suppliers of raw materials, or reduce levels of stocks towards 'zero stocks', i.e. raw materials only delivered as required for the day, no work-in-progress, and products made only to order and for immediate delivery resulting in flexibility [see Topic 7 Operations management, p. 85 JIT].

- Tighten up credit control, checking beforehand that potential customers *can* pay, and chasing them up afterwards to make sure they *do* pay – soon! Late payments, particularly by large businesses to small businesses, has been such a problem that the Labour Government considered legislation, e.g. allowing interest to be charged on late payments.

- Use **factoring**, i.e. loans (usually 80%) from a factoring company directly based on the value of invoices issued to customers. In spite of the fee, and interest charged, this could reduce administration costs and increase the flexibility of financing the working capital (especially if there is a direct computer link for the transactions).

A business needs a continual supply of cash, and enough **liquid assets** (i.e. close to cash), to meet likely demands of creditors (i.e. those owed money).

Cashflow

A business which is **insolvent** (i.e. cannot meet its debts) may be forced to go into **liquidation** (i.e. have its assets all sold off), if the creditors decide to call in debts owed to them (e.g. a bank loan, or the costs of supplies of raw materials).

> *'Businesses typically fail because they run out of cash, not because they report accounting losses.'*
>
> Professor Keith Ward, *Financial Aspects of Marketing* (1989).

> *'If cashflow analysis techniques had been used by the bankers responsible for the Laker Airways account [see p. 99 Gearing], they ought to have become worried in 1978...,*
>
> T. A. Lee, 'Laker Airways, the cashflow truth', *Accountancy* (6/92).

Lack of cash is usually due to problems of financing working capital, e.g. a time difference between paying bills and receiving payments. A 'cashflow crisis' is where the availability of cash is exhausted (due to inaccurate forecasting or unexpected events, e.g. a customer's business goes into liquidation). A large business paying late can have serious knock-on effects on the cashflow of the smaller businesses it buys from.

Improving cashflow

- Reduce the time cash is tied up before final products are sold
- Spread purchase costs
- Use factoring (i.e. 'sell' invoices)
- Delay payments (of invoices)!

- Tighten stock control
- Tighten credit control (of debtors)
- Sell assets and lease them back
- Reduce the level of investment
- Plan – using cashflow forecasts.

Cashflow forecasts (or budgets) are an essential tool of planning,

E.g. for a new product – link with the product life-cycle (p. 60).

e.g.	£000s (Negative figures in brackets)						
	Jan	Feb	Mar	Apr	May	Jun	
Sales	6	6	8	8	11	12	[e.g. half cash, half on credit]
Cash sales	3	3	4	4	5.5	6	[e.g. half of sales revenue]
Cash: credit sales [Dec]	4	3	3	4	4	5.5	[e.g. half of *last* month's sales]
Total inflow	7	6	7	8	9.5	11.5	
Outflow Stock	2.5	2.5	2.5	2	2.1		
Labour	2	2	2	2	2		
Rent	2	–	–	2	–		[quarterly bills/payments]
Electricity	0.5	–	–	0.5	–		[quarterly bills/payments]
Advertising	–	0.3	–	0.3			[not every month for some reason]
Interest	0.5	0.5	0.5	0.6			[extra overdraft in April?]
Total outflow	7.5	5.3	5	7.4			
Net cashflow	(0.5)	(0.7)	2	0.6			[*total inflow* MINUS *total outflow*]
Opening balance [Dec]	(0.5)	(1)	(0.3)	1.7			[last month's closing balance]
Closing balance	(1)	(0.3)	1.7	2.3			[next month's opening balance]

Some businesses are 'cash-rich' e.g. railways – people pay at the time or even in advance (for season tickets).

Cashflow forecasts can be used to predict periods of cash shortage (when additional finance is needed [see Topic 6 Marketing, p. 60 Product life-cycle – 'Death Valley Ride'], or cash surpluses (for profitable use), and in assessing new projects with forecasts amended as performance data becomes available).

Cashflow statements include all inflows and outflows of cash for the (past) period covered. Not all flows are included in the profit and loss account.

The accounts

- Record past performance.
- State present position.
- Indicate future prospects.

Several stakeholders would be interested in a business's performance:

- the owners
- customers/clients
- creditors

- managers
- other employees
- competitors

- Financial advisors
- local community
- the government.

To assess the performance, it is necessary to have financial information in a recognisable and understandable form...The two main elements in the accounts are:

(i) The balance sheet

This is a snapshot (or similar to a car's milometer) which shows the financial situation of a business at a particular time (e.g. the end of the financial year), and answers two basic questions about the business:

- where did the resources come from?
- where are those resources now?

It lists all assets (owned by the business) and subtracts liabilities (amounts owed in that year). The resulting 'net assets employed', i.e. what has been done with the finance put into the business, must equal/balance 'capital employed', i.e. the total amount of long-term finance invested in the business since it started.

What needs to balance?

What size business is this?

How can you tell it must be a limited company?

e.g.

As at 31st December 1998:			£000	(Negatives in brackets)
Fixed assets:	Land and buildings		240	[Least-liquid assets]
	Plant and machinery	485		
	Depreciation	(125)		
			360	
Current assets:	Stock	150		
	Debtors	96		
	Cash	24		[Most-liquid assets]
		270		
minus current liabilities:				
	Creditors	123		
	Dividends payable	47		
		170		
Working capital	Net current assets		100	
	Net assets employed		700*	[*Must be equal]
Financed by:	Share capital		450	
	Reserves		90	
	Bank loan		160	
	Capital employed		700*	[*Must be equal]

NB Long-term liabilities (i.e. the £160,000 bank loan) are often deducted from the total of assets (£240,000 + £360,000 + £100,000), and, this figure (£540,000) will equal the 'financing' from shares and reserves.

- **Fixed assets** – resources not regularly sold by the business, e.g. land, buildings, plant and equipment, which are 'tangible' assets. Depreciation (an estimate of annual costs of wear and tear on assets, and then replacement) needs to be deducted from their value. 'Intangible' assets, e.g. investment in R and D, ownership of a well-known brand name or patent, and goodwill, may be more difficult to value but are needed for a true 'snapshot'.

- **Current assets** – resources expected to be converted into cash during the current financial year, including stocks, debtors (minus provision for bad debts), shares in subsidiaries, and cash itself.

- **Current liabilities** – debts where repayment is due within the current year, including overdrafts, raw materials bought on credit, insurance premiums, taxes, and dividends distributed to shareholders.

- **Share capital** – long-term finance raised by issuing shares, up to the maximum amount authorised by shareholders. They would have to agree (by majority vote) to any increase.

- **Reserves** – mainly accumulated retained profits (not distributed to shareholders), but can also include share 'premiums' (where they have been sold above face value) and asset revaluations (e.g. if buildings rise in value).

(ii) The profit and loss account

Unlike the balance sheet 'snapshot', this measures performance over a period of time (like a car's speedometer). Data for at least the previous time period will usually be included, for comparisons which can show the trends in the profitability of the business. Again, there are two elements:

- **Revenue** – income from selling the product good or service, including customers' cash payments and the debts/amounts owing.

- **Expenses** – costs of production during the particular time period, split into direct and indirect costs, or fixed and variable costs [see Topic 7 Operations management, p. 76 Costs of production].

e.g. An abbreviated Profit and Loss Account of a small business...

	1997	1998
Sales revenue	£ 210,000	£ 284,000
Minus direct costs:		
Raw materials/components	92,000	106,000
Labour	53,000	64,000
Gross profit	65,000	114,000
Minus indirect costs:		
Interest	14,000	15,000
Overheads	15,000	18,000
Depreciation	10,000	10,000
Net profit (or loss) before tax	26,000	71,000

The profit and loss [P&L] account can give an accurate picture of the trends in a firm's profitability but, on its own, cannot give a full picture of overall performance.

E.g. If a limited company took over another company, of similar size and profit levels, and paid for the acquisition by an issue of new shares. If, in the following year, profits almost doubled, the performance of the business may not have improved – if the number of shares doubled (after the new issue) the 'earnings per share' [see p. 104 The primary ratios] may not have changed at all (or it may even have fallen).

Ratios

- Used to analyse business performance.

- In several forms, e.g. ½, 2:1, 9%.

- A ratio needs a base from which to compare – internally from a previous year, or externally from a norm amongst competitors.

Not an exhaustive list. A case study might suggest another ratio is calculable.

- Several 'performance' ratios involve comparing information from the balance sheet with that from the profit and loss account, while other 'liquidity' ratios can be calculated just from balance sheets.

The primary ratio:

$$\text{Return on Capital Employed (ROCE)} = \frac{\text{net profit [P\&L]}}{\text{capital employed [BS]}} \times 100$$

Also expressed as Return on Net Assets (RONA), it can be used for opportunity cost decisions on whether a business is worth investing in at the moment, i.e. What has it done with each £1 invested? What was the risk involved? Would a bank, building society or government gilt-edged securities 'gilts' have given a similar or better % return, with little risk?

$$\text{Net Asset Turnover (NAT)} = \frac{\text{sales [P\&L]}}{\text{net assets [BS]}}$$

How effectively have the assets been used by the managers in the business?

$$\text{Earnings Per Share (EPS)} = \frac{\text{net profit after tax [P\&L]}}{\text{number of shares [BS]}}$$

How has the business performed for the shareholders/owners? The ratio will take account of any change in the number of shares (e.g. after a rights issue among existing shareholders).

$$\text{Price/Earnings Ratio (P/E)} = \frac{\text{market price of the share}}{\text{EPS}}$$

What is the market's view of the future potential performance of the business? A high ratio (e.g. 30+) indicates buyers are prepared to pay a much higher price for each share than the return currently being provided for shareholders.

$$\text{Current Ratio} = \frac{\text{current assets [BS]}}{\text{current liabilities [BS]}}$$

A broad measure of the liquidity of the business, and whether it could manage if all or most creditors suddenly wanted repayment. A 'cash rich' business may have a ratio of around one, while a heavy-equipment manufacturer may have one of five, but a ratio of two is seen as encouraging because assets, e.g. some stock, may not be quickly converted into cash.

$$\text{Acid Test Ratio [or Quick Assets Ratio]} = \frac{\text{current assets minus stock [BS]}}{\text{current liabilities [BS]}}$$

This more stringent/testing measure leaves out stock which, in some cases, could take time to convert to cash. Short-term debts are included because most can be turned into cash, e.g. by factoring. A ratio around one usually confirms that there are no obvious liquidity problems.

$$\text{Stock Turnover} = \frac{\text{cost of sales [P\&L]}}{\text{stocks [BS]}}$$

A measure of how well working capital is being managed. A high ratio, e.g. 2+, might suggest efforts have been made to keep stocks to a minimum [see Topic 7 Operations management, p. 85 Stocks] but, if coupled with a low Acid Test Ratio (e.g. <1), it might indicate that the business could not rely on selling stock to pay off short-term debts.

$$\text{Gearing} = \frac{\text{long-term liabilities or debts [BS]}}{\text{capital employed [BS]}}$$

Find out the current % return on gilts, and from a building society.

As in the financial pages of share prices.

There are variations on this formula, but all versions compare the amount of capital raised by borrowing, to that raised by issuing shares [see p. 99 Gearing].

> *'For the private sector, the key attraction of owning a passenger rail franchise is to get your hands on the cashflow. Much of that comes as pre-payments for season tickets, and analysts estimate that Stagecoach will inherit some £48 million of cash when it takes over the South West Trains (SWT) franchise, providing a very useful reduction in the bus company's gearing.'*
>
> The Times (21/12/95).

Ratios, usually in combination with other ratios or data, are useful for evaluating a firm's performance, compared to previous years or to other businesses. They may warn of problems, or suggest areas for improvement, but:

- ratios are only as reliable as the data from which they are calculated

- some data, e.g. stock, may be subjectively defined

- comparisons between businesses may be difficult, due to different year-ends, different product-mixes, different objectives, or different accounting methods – although standardisation is becoming more usual

- historic information used, and the future may not reflect past trends

- only financial data used to measure performance – no other market information.

Good for evaluation.

Depreciation

This is the amount deducted each year, on the Balance Sheet, as 'fixed assets' (e.g. vehicles) wear out, lose value, need maintenance and then, after some specified time period, need replacing.

A **fixed asset**, e.g. a new computer system designed to last for five years, could be 'written off' against the Profit and Loss Account for that year, or it could be written off in its last year before being replaced. Both of these would distort the true picture (possibly turning a year's profit into a loss) if, as is usual, the asset is productive for the business over several years, so businesses normally write off an asset over the whole of its expected useful life.

Could an asset appreciate in value? In what circumstances?

To calculate depreciation of a fixed asset, a business needs:

- original cost/value of the asset

- expected useful life (e.g. four years for PCs)

- expected scrap or residual value

- a method...   [gradients!]

Straight-line

This simpler method (used by most UK companies), divides the total cost to be written off (i.e. purchase cost of asset minus likely scrap or residual value) by the expected useful life. The resulting amount is deducted each year from the 'Net Book Value (NBV)' of the asset as in the accounts. The NBV will fall by equal amounts each year.

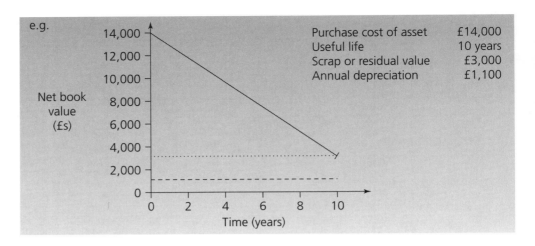

e.g.

Purchase cost of asset	£14,000
Useful life	10 years
Scrap or residual value	£3,000
Annual depreciation	£1,100

Declining balance

E.g. a vehicle.

This more complicated method (apparently used by most US companies), has a higher rate of depreciation in the earlier years of the asset's life, in order to give a more accurate representation of a declining market value. The NBV falls by an equal percentage each year, and the residual value is reached at the end of the asset's useful life.

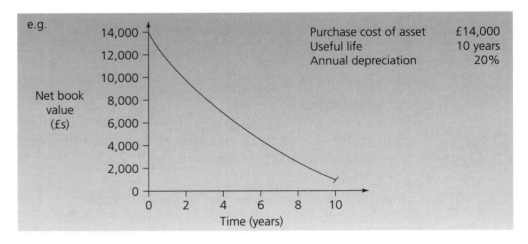

e.g.

Purchase cost of asset	£14,000
Useful life	10 years
Annual depreciation	20%

Investment appraisal

Should the business invest in a new venture/project?

Investment could be in property, capital equipment, R and D [see Topic 7 Operations management], a training project [see Topic 5 Human resource management], or a new marketing project [see Topic 6 Marketing]. There may be a range of alternative investments [see Topic 8 Data and Information Technology, p. 93 Decision trees], and decisions can be based on a range of qualitative factors, e.g.

- predicted trends in the economy and the level of business confidence

- the degree of ambition to expand, – perhaps to diversify to spread risks.

There are quantitative ones as well – the three main methods of appraisal assume the overriding objective is profit.

(i) Payback

The payback period is the length of time needed for the cost of an investment to be recovered, by the 'net cashflow' – any increase in cash inflows (e.g. increased sales) or decrease in outflows (e.g. savings in labour or raw material costs) e.g.

(a) A new four-year advertising campaign costing £40,000, to increase sales and capture a greater market share. Market research suggested these results:

Year	Net cashflows (from increased sales)
1	£25,000
2	£15,000
3	£10,000
4	£5,000

...the payback period would be two years.

(b) Choosing between two new computer systems, both costing £45,000 each. It has been calculated that:

System A will cut costs by £10,000 in year 1, £20,000 in year 2 and £30,000 in year 3.

System B gives savings of £30,000 in year 1, £20,000 in year 2 and £10,000 in year 3.

The payback periods are in year 3 for System A, and in year 2 for System B.

On the face of it, the faster payback will be preferred because of the reduced risks, and funds will then be available earlier for other expenditure.

(ii) Average rate of return

The ARR compares likely returns with cost outlay, e.g.

A printing business considering whether to buy a new £200,000 machine – a significant investment for them but, apparently, over its five-year life there would also be significant savings in labour and materials.

Year	Cashflow
1	£55,000
2	£60,000
3	£65,000
4	£70,000
5	£75,000

To calculate ARR:

Total cash contribution over lifetime	£325,000
Total lifetime profit (i.e. after deduction of cost outlay)	£125,000
Average annual profit (i.e. divide profit by no. of years)	£25,000

$$\frac{\text{Average annual profit}}{\text{The total cost of the investment}} \times 100 = \frac{25,000}{200,000} \times 100 = 12.5\%$$

How does this return compare with alternative investments?

(iii) Net present value

The NPV allows a more accurate comparison between costs of an investment project and all future returns by converting all the amounts into 'present values', e.g. allowing for likely effects of inflation. A discount rate will be used – in a sense the opposite of compound interest.

If the interest rate is 10%, then in three years' time £1 will be worth (with compound interest) £1 x 110% x 110% x 110% = £1.33.

If the discount rate is 10%, then in three years' time £1 will only be worth (after dividing by 110%) £1 – 110% – 110% – 110% = £0.75.

A business is deciding whether to invest in a new £30,000 machine. Their accountant uses a 10% discount rate to calculate 'present values', to give an idea of likely real returns:

	Cash inflows	Discount factor	Present value
Year 1:	£8,000	0.909	£7,272
Year 2:	£8,000	0.826	£6,608
Year 3:	£8,000	0.751	£6,008
Year 4:	£8,000	0.683	£5,464
Year 5:	£8,000	0.621	£4,968
	£40,000		£30,320

The surplus (£40,000 minus the £30,000 cost of the project) initially seems to be £10,000, but the 'discounted' surplus (£30,320 minus the cost of the project) is only £320 – quite a difference!

Advantages:
- overcomes the problem of comparing 'present/current' money and 'future' money
- results of the analysis are easily compared.

Disadvantages:
- more complicated initially, as forecasts have to be made about interest rates and discount rates
- no account taken of the returns from investing the cash inflows.

External influences

Population

Some of these, e.g. UK and EU legislation have been included elsewhere, when relevant.

UK population rose by <2% 1980–1990, and as slowly during the 1990s. The official forecast is for a rise (from 57 million in 1990) to 60 million by 2025 – not a fast growth rate historically or compared to other industrialised nations. The average 230 people per sq. km of land area is not defined as 'overpopulated'. More important to businesses are the trends within the national totals.

Age distribution

This relates to the number of people in each age group. With a fall in the birth rate, after the 1950–1970 baby-boom (peaking in 1964), and a more gradually reducing death rate, the average age of the UK population has increased and the country has become an ageing population. In 1996 the bulge in the distribution of the population was between the ages 26–46; by 2025 it will be at the 55–75 age range – the government forecast that the retired population would reach 38.5% of working-age population by 2025 (29.4% in 1985). Numbers of people in that working-age group is forecast to remain roughly static at just under 35 million, giving a significantly increased **Dependency ratio**:

Can you work out the formula?

$$\text{Dependency ratio} = \frac{\text{Total population}}{\text{Number of people in work}}$$

Demand-side – customers

Which kind of businesses are affected?

- Manufacturers of toys deciding whether board games will be more profitable than bricks for toddlers.
- Soft drink manufacturers whose market research suggests some younger adults have 'cola fatigue'.
- Fashion clothing shops deciding whether to switch from targeting teenagers – a million in the early 1980s but <750,000 by the 1990s, to designs appealing to women in their 20s – now the main target group.
- Car producers reacting (e.g. with new interior designs) to a third of new cars being purchased by the over-50 age in 1995.
- The pensions industry, with the over-50s controlling over 70% of UK savings by 1995 – much more marketing in evidence by the late 1990s. In 1931 a man's life expectancy was 60; by 1996 it had risen to 73 with, on average women living even longer.

Supply-side – workers

- The lower birth rate after 1970 and more 16-year-olds staying on for Further Education (FE) meant that, by the mid-1980s the number of teenagers leaving school, and looking for jobs, fell sharply. In 1986 there were 6.2 million people aged 16–24, and by 1996 the number fell further, to 4.8 million, affecting businesses, e.g. banks and large retail chains, used to recruiting staff straight from school, or in their early 20s.

In 1990 Marks and Spencer plc gave shop staff a 26% pay increase to reduce labour turnover, particularly of younger workers.

In 1991 the DIY store B and Q opened a new store in Macclesfield staffed by 'mature' workers (over 50).

- The 1990–93 recession changed the labour market again. Many businesses saw the extra costs of retaining staff as unnecessary, when they could recruit cheaply from unemployed labour, or increase productivity and make redundancies.

Regional distribution

Significant changes in the distribution of the sexes in the UK population are rarer.

This relates to where people live. Most UK citizens live in seven 'conurbations' (with London's population equal to that of Australia!), but with a trend towards moving out into smaller towns and the countryside. This is partly due to improved transport enabling commuting, and larger numbers of retired people wanting to move. Some sociologists have predicted an increasing trend towards **home-working**, because of advances in Information Technology (IT).

'Between 1989 and 2011 the population of East Anglia is projected to increase by 16% (from 2.04 million to 2.38 million) and that of the South-West by 15% (from 4.65 million to 5.34 million). The projections are based on estimates for local and health authority areas which have been analysed by sex and age... Only two regions are expected to show a population decrease; the North, down 2%, and the North-West, down 1%.'

Office of Population, Censuses and Surveys (12/91).

Occupational distribution

This relates to the production sectors in which people work, e.g. percentages in 1995:

	Primary	Secondary	Tertiary
UK	3	38	59
USA	4	30	66
France	9	35	56
Spain	17	37	46
Greece	31	29	40
Turkey	58	17	25
India	70	13	17

The UK economy suffers from 'deindustrialisation' usually defined as a decline in manufacturing employment. Data confirms that the expanding tertiary sector has not managed to soak up the redundancies from manufacturing, so, after the early 1980s, the overall level of UK unemployment rose significantly.

Culture

What represents British culture? Would an international marketing campaign help UK competitiveness?

Every society has a culture – something that embodies that group of people's particular perceptions, beliefs, standards/norms.

'There is a deeply rooted anti-industrial culture in the UK. As with all crises, it requires leadership from all sectors of the community, with government at the head, to harness the skills and efforts of the country to the central objective of improving our productive capacity, without which we can do nothing for ourselves or others.'

Sir Geoffrey Chandler, Director-General of The National Economic Development Office (1984).

The government announced 1986 (and then 1987!) as 'Industry Year', to attempt to improve the image of manufacturing, particularly among school leavers and university graduates.

The prevailing culture in a society, or community, will be very important to businesses, as they target consumers [see Topic 6 Marketing, p. 58], and employ people [see Topic 5 Human resource management].

- **The Single Market** (officially open for business from 1st January 1993) is an attempt to reduce all main trade barriers between (EU) member countries, with a total population greater than the USA and Japan combined! However, barriers to trade remain, e.g. different exchange rates (until a single currency applies to all members), different languages and different cultures.

Within the national culture there are identifiable subcultures, determined by sex, race, religion, socio-economic groups [see Topic 6 Marketing] and geographical factors, and which will also be important for businesses to consider, e.g. on food products.

A business will have its own culture (influenced by the national culture) – a code, unwritten or perhaps contained in a 'mission statement', that affects attitudes, decision-making and management style [see Topic 4 Management]. Different types include:

- goal-orientated – bonus-seeking, youthful, and emphasising success

- hierarchical – based on respect for seniority, tight communication and avoidance of mistakes

- growth-orientated – lively and based on commitment to the product and shared values/'corporatism'

- person-orientated – based on meeting the needs of individual employees.

[See Topic 2 Objectives and Topic 4 Management and leadership, p. 13 Blake's Grid].

Management may become concerned that the culture of their organisation is inappropriate or even resistant to changes required by a changing economic environment.

Ethics

These are moral principles that underpin decision-making, i.e. questions of 'right or wrong', and follow on from a society's or organisation's culture. A business decision made on ethical grounds might be to reject the most profitable solution in favour of one of greater benefit to society (including the firm itself). There is usually a subjective element to questions, e.g.

How much of an ethical dilemma would the following represent?

- Should a firm help its own cashflow, but harm the cashflow of a smaller business, by delaying payment of a debt?

- Should an advertising agency accept a cigarette manufacturer as a client?

- Should a business allow 'exploitative advertising' to be used to sell one of its products (e.g. to tackle 'Generation X' consumers)?

- Should a business which has to cut costs to survive (e.g. in a deep recession) consider cutting expenditure on the reduction of noise or effluent pollution?

- Should an employee of 30 years' standing, who has been warned several times about his performance at work, but is unlikely to get a job elsewhere, be made redundant?

- Should a bank make loans to a company selling arms?

- Should a firm on the end of a hostile takeover bid employ private detectives to investigate the private lives of the bidding company's directors?

What about your part of the world?

Examples?

Ask a few other people, of different ages, male and female? Is there bias in the way the question is asked?

And there are plenty of others. Are the decisions more difficult if a great deal of money is involved?

The first course in business ethics was offered by Harvard University in 1915, but it is only since the mid-1980s that the business ethics movement has shown significant growth. In 1990 it was estimated that one in three of leading UK companies has published a code of ethics.

Pressure groups, including the media and consumer groups, have played a part, along with subsequent legislation, in ethical issues becoming more prominent in business thinking, e.g. on the environment.

A piece of marketing as well?

Sir,

Socially responsible businesses are encouraged and delighted by the growing power of ethical consumers. This rapidly growing movement of animal welfarists and human rights and environmental activists is rightly waking up to the role of business in abusing the environment and people... Let's celebrate the fact that business, which today is more powerful than most governments, is having to adopt a sustainable agenda respecting the earth and its people, rather than one that will literally cost the earth.

Yours sincerely,
Gavin Grant

(General Manager Global Public Affairs, Body Shop International plc)

Letter to *The Times* (11/2/97)

Legislation such as the Clean Air Act 1956 and the Control of Pollution Act 1974 were government responses to growing environmental problems, such as 'smog'. During the 1980s, public concern and pressure grew noticeably over issues such as acid rain, toxic waste and global warming, e.g.:

- A dramatic fall in demand for aerosol products using chlorofluorocarbons (CFCs), and butane-propelled hairspray sales rising 250% in the early 1980s. ICI developed hydrogen-based gases to replace chlorine-based CFCs used in refrigerators, and IBM stopped using CFC solvents for cleaning circuit boards.

In 1989 500 large companies, including IBM, National Power, J. Laing, National Westminster Bank, Coca-Cola and J. Sainsbury, joined the national 'Business in the Community' initiative, to show that voluntary action by business leaders would bring more long-term benefits to the nation than legislation on its own.

In 1991 The British Standards Institute (BSI) published an official national standard, the first in the world, for quality of environmental management. A business has to have a detailed policy, implemented from boardroom to shopfloor, and comply with, or exceed, current regulations.

See also Topic 7 Operations management, p. 87 Quality.

'...A company which cannot boast the BSI logo on environmental performance will be at a competitive disadvantage. Big investors might be suspicious that a company which has not complied is concealing environmental liabilities which could hamper its profits and performance.'

Financial Times (11/91).

There has also gradually been more strict legislation, e.g. Environmental Protection Act 1990 and several EU directives, for businesses to observe.

Sustainable development integrates economic growth and business efficiency, to protect and enhance the environment and resources for future generations. In 1992 the Confederation of British Industry (CBI) launched its 'Environmental Business Forum', to create a network that could provide local guidance on environmental management to all sizes of companies in any type of business sector. A growing number of companies see competitive advantages to projecting a 'green'/caring image, and include it in their marketing strategy [see Topic 6 Marketing].

The economic environment

(a) The market

Businesses have to monitor and analyse their markets continuously, to be market-led (rather than product-led).

See p. 60 Product life-cycle.

- The American market for trainers fell 50% between 1996 and 1998. (Still 'one-in-five pairs' of shoes sold in the UK market in 1998, though.)

- In 1997 British women spent £13.6 billion in the fashion clothing market, while men spent £6.4 billion, an average of 'only' £250 a year each [Source: MINTEL].

A market is where buyers' **demand** meets producers' **supply** – these 'market forces' determine the market price for the good or service. There could be government intervention, e.g. an increase in a relevant tax to discourage supply and/or demand, or a subsidy or grant to encourage supply.

Think of examples all the way through this topic, or use examples from a case study in an exam paper.

- In 1998 the road haulage company Eddie Stobart Ltd was awarded a £20 million grant to fund its move into freight transport.

The market (or price) mechanism

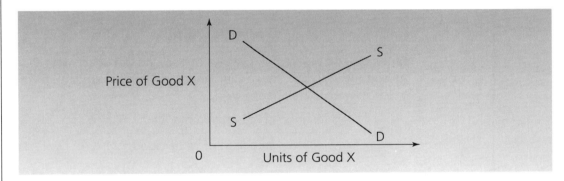

- The higher the price the lower the quantity demanded – usually.

- The higher the price the more producers will want to supply – usually.

- Market equilibrium – where demand equals supply, setting the market price – only for that precise time though!

Changes in demand

In the analysis of markets, there is an important difference between movement along a demand curve and movement to a new demand curve. There is only one possible cause of a change in the quantity demanded (shown by a movement along the curve) – a price change:

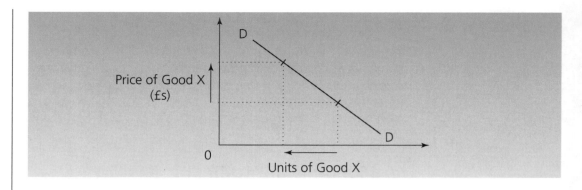

Before a business alters the price of one of its goods or services, it will gauge the likely responsiveness/reaction of customers – measured by **price elasticity of demand**:

$$\text{PED} = \frac{\% \text{ Change in quantity demanded}}{\% \text{ Change in price}}$$

$$\% \text{ change in the quantity demanded} = \frac{\text{Change in quantity demanded x 100}}{\text{Original quantity demanded}}$$

$$\% \text{ change in the price} = \frac{\text{Change in price x 100}}{\text{Original price}}$$

The formula will provide a 'coefficient' (usually negative):

PED >1 means 'elastic'/responsive demand, and **Total Revenue** (TR) will rise after a price decrease, but fall after a price increase.

PED <1 means 'inelastic'/unresponsive demand, and TR will increase after a price increase but reduce it in the case of a price decrease.

• What does 'PED = 1' mean?...TR will stay the same in this case?

Other types of elasticity of demand:

Cross-elasticity – responsiveness of demand between two products, e.g. they could be substitutes (e.g. butter and margarine), or complements (e.g. cameras and film), or have no strong link/correlation:

$$\text{CED} = \frac{\% \text{ change in quantity demanded of Good X}}{\% \text{ change in price of Good Y}}$$

Income elasticity – responsiveness of consumers to changes in their income. For most products demand increases as incomes rise, except for inferior goods:

$$\text{IED} = \frac{\% \text{ change in quantity demanded of Good X}}{\% \text{ change in income}}$$

Advertising elasticity – the extent to which consumers respond to an advertising spend.

Taxation can affect incomes and the prices of particular products (e.g. cigarettes), so the Chancellor of the Exchequer and economists, as well as the affected businesses, will often have an interest in the various coefficients of elasticity.

There are several possible determinants of a change in demand – shown by movement to a new curve, i.e. people feel differently about the product, for one or more reasons.

...So 'elasticity' (of any type) measures responsiveness to change.

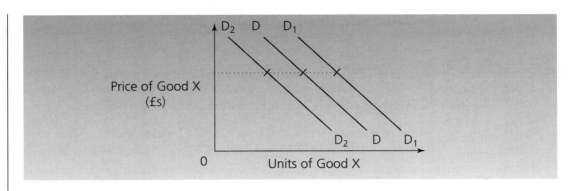

- DD is the original level of demand, so D_1D_1 represents an overall increase in demand for Good X, and D_2D_2 shows the effect of a fall in demand.

Determinants of a change in demand

- **Population** – nationally or locally [see p. 109 Population: Demand-side]

- **Disposable incomes** – rising (on average) in most years, and several products previously labelled as 'luxuries' may become common in UK households.

- **Publicity** – including expenditure on advertising to boost or even create demand, and bad publicity, e.g. from experts predicting falls in share prices or heightening concern over BSE, significantly reducing demand.

- **Seasons** – e.g. for products related to religious festivals, or certain weather. New methods of storage and transportation have made availability of some perishables (e.g. fruit and vegetables) less seasonal.

- **Derived demand** – e.g. Demand for video cassettes stems from the demand for video cassette recorders [see 'Cross-elasticity']. The demand for a type of worker (e.g. in professional sport) usually derives from the demand for the product he or she is involved with.

Take a particular good or service, e.g. from an exam case study.

Changes in supply

There are several possible causes of a change in supply, i.e. producers becoming more (or less) willing to supply their products to the market – shown by a new supply curve:

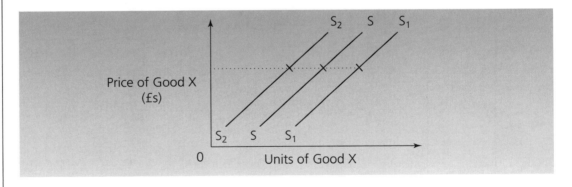

- SS is the original level of supply, so S_1S_1 represents an overall increase in supply for Good X, and S_2S_2 shows the effect of a fall in supply.

(Price) elasticity of supply measures how producers/suppliers will respond to changes in market prices:

$$PES = \frac{\% \text{ change in quantity supplied}}{\% \text{ change in price}}$$

(The coefficient is calculated in the same way as for price elasticity of demand.)

Determinants of a change in supply

Take a particular good or service, e.g. from an exam case study.

- **Time** – e.g. a newly-designed car takes time to supply from inception to the finished products being available for purchase, and therefore risks may be greater. What price will customers accept when the product does reach the market? The longer the period of time, the more responsive producers can be.

- **Expectations** – e.g. for some crops (which, again, may take some time to come to the market), where the suppliers take note of previous price trends.

- **Climate and weather** – e.g. longer- or short-term changes affecting supply conditions, e.g. in oil exploration, fishing or sport. Temperature changes may affect the extent of agricultural crop diseases or pollution.

- **Technology** – e.g. automation may allow further economies of scale, e.g. in car production or horticulture, and thus encourage supply. For certain products supply can only be economic if demand is sufficient for mass production.

- **Factors of production** – e.g. a rise in the price of a crucial raw material, or the low availability or high price of essential labour, could discourage supply. The availability and price/interest-rate of investment capital would also be important.

- **Alternative products** – e.g. a farmer switching from a crop to one that receives a better EU subsidy, or a producer switching to a product that is believed to provide a more secure long-term demand.

- **Government** – e.g. grants or subsidies to encourage supply in an area of high unemployment, or of an important food product (e.g. milk). 'Intellectual property' [see Topic 7 Operations management, p. 75] legislation may encourage the supply of new products. UK and EU legislation on health and safety, or the environment may restrict output of particular goods and services. Taxation can also affect supply, e.g. the effects of an indirect tax such as VAT.

How much of the tax can a business pass on to customers? It is a question of **relative (price) elasticities of demand and supply**:

For which product, for example?

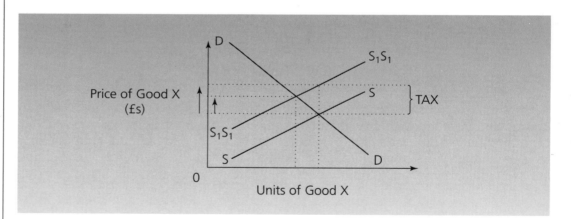

Label these...

- SS is the original supply curve, and S_1S_1 is the curve after the tax is imposed or increased.

Where is the original 'equilibrium' before the tax is put on?

What is the new equilibrium price paid by customers with the tax put on?

How much tax will be absorbed by producers, e.g. by lower profits?

In what situation can a business pass on most, if not all, of the tax?

Which curve is steeper? What would happen if relative gradients were changed?

Not all of the tax would be passed on – unless demand would be unresponsive to a price change i.e. $E_d = 0$.

(b) The economy

Businesses are part of the economic trends within an economy, and are in turn affected by those trends.

> 'Tony Blair is to publish a company-style report on "UK plc" in May, to mark the Government's first anniversary in power. The report will detail targets for the year, and whether they have been achieved...It will not be audited by external auditors...It is not clear whether Mr Blair will style himself chairman or chief executive, or ignore the Cadbury code on corporate governance and claim both titles.'
>
> The Times (23/4/98).

Types of economy

- **Traditional economy** – There will tend to be (relatively) low production, according to individuals' subsistence needs, and thus a low average standard of living. A government might encourage its economy to develop.

- **Command economy** – Production decisions are taken by a central economic authority (e.g. in the former USSR), with production based on a limited range of products across the whole economy, according to the needs of the population. Theoretically, effective planning of economies of scale could provide **efficiency** of production.

- **Market economy** – Production decisions are taken by producers reacting to the demand in the market. Theoretically, the resulting competition benefits the consumer by providing more **choice** from a wide range of products. Several ex-Communist Bloc countries have set out to develop market economies (and perhaps, in the future, aim to join the Single Market).

- Inevitably there will be a mixture of politics and economics in such important decisions affecting a whole society.

- The UK economy can also be described as a **mixed economy** – a mixture of private and public sectors [see Topic 1 Types of businesses].

How many government departments can you name? How many ministers?

Economic objectives

For a developed economy the overall objectives will normally include:

- increasing standard of living
- stable prices
- high level of employment
- favourable international trade
- distribution of income.

[See Topic 2 Objectives, p. 7 Governments].

Look in newspapers for the current trends, to impress the examiners with your depth of understanding.

How an economy works

To understand and explain, a simple model can be used, including just two sectors – households/consumers and businesses):

Why make it complicated?

The circular flow of income

Use the (American) KISS principle (Keep It Simple, Stupid!).

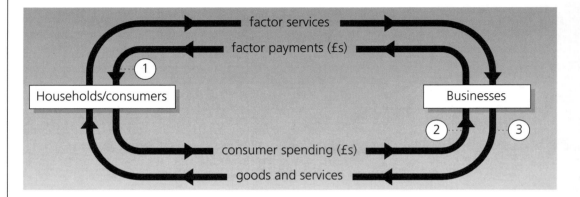

The thickness/volume of the flow will be **the level of economic activity**, and there are three gauges (similar to those on a car dashboard):

① **National income** – sum of all the household's income from providing their labour, land, and capital i.e. 'risk-taking'.

② **National expenditure** – total spending by consumers, on businesses' products.

③ **National product** – total value of the production of the businesses in the economy.

- The three gauges/measures should give the same total (because they are measuring the same 'flow'). In practice, the complex collation of all the data means differences, but data from one can still be useful as a check for accuracy of another.

- Once the simple model is understood, other sectors could be added (with their appropriate 'flows', i.e. the government and international trade sectors. Exports will cause an inflow of funds to the economy (and imports cause an outflow of funds, into the circular flow of another economy).

- The third gauge, often expressed as 'Gross National Product', is the usual measure taken for a nation's standard of living. ('Gross Domestic Product' will not include, for example, income from a UK company's production abroad.)

Business cycles

Economies are dynamic, i.e. continually changing, and the economic changes will affect individuals, businesses and governments. Economists have identified patterns of economic activity, called **business (or trade or economic) cycles**, i.e. recovery → boom → recession → slump → recovery →

Spot the deep recessions?

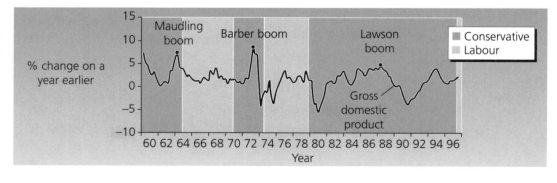

When will the next recession and then boom arrive? With what effects?

Forecasting trends is complex, e.g. recessions do not occur regularly every five years, but hopefully the long-term overall trend will be economic growth, giving an increasing standard of living per capita.

- What evidence is there that the standard of living has risen over the last 25 years?

Governments, businesses and some individuals are particularly interested in the causes, timing and effects of the cycles. To some extent, markets within the economy may be affected differently, e.g. a recovery officially began in summer 1993, but only by summer 1996 were most (still not all) parts of the UK housing market showing signs of increasing demand and prices not falling.

Recession

- Officially two consecutive quarters of GDP falling, e.g. 1990–93.

Problems:

- lower levels of consumer spending/demand in most markets
- unemployment, as businesses cut production and make workers redundant
- many businesses cut back on investment – 'the key to future growth'!
- more business liquidations
- business confidence falls (perhaps lengthening the recession period).

But...

- less 'demand-pull' inflation – interest rates may be allowed to fall
- fewer imports are sucked in (helping flows on the Balance of Payments)
- businesses which survive may have been forced to become leaner and fitter.

Recovery

- Officially two consecutive quarters of GDP rising, e.g. 1993–98.

Advantages:

- higher levels of consumer spending/demand in most markets
- profits rise and businesses (with the capacity) raise production
- employment opportunities if businesses raise production
- businesses more prepared to take business risks and invest in new projects
- fewer business liquidations
- business confidence rises (perhaps lengthening the recovery period).

Disadvantages:

- inflation will start to rise – requiring policy action, e.g. interest rate rises
- more imports are sucked in (hindering flows on the Balance of Payments)
- businesses may not have the capacity to respond to the increased demand.

So a government would be concerned that a recession does not go too low or for too long, but on the other hand, that a boom (e.g. 'the Lawson boom' 1988–89) does not go too high – that too can cause economic (and political!) problems.

> 'You can't please awl of the people awl of the time.'
>
> Abraham Lincoln (1862).

The policies

The Chancellor has a group of advisors (whose advice may often be 'On the one hand, Minister,... However, on the other hand...'!), and also regular monthly meetings with the Governor of the Bank of England. The Bank has its finger on the pulse of financial markets.

When is the next (UK) cycle due?

Is it always possible to keep the economics and politics separate?

Fancy the job of Chancellor?

Demand-management policies

Economists and politicians who emphasise spending as the main determinant of the performance of an economy, are often referred to as **Keynesians**.

John Maynard Keynes revolutionised thinking on **macroeconomics**, i.e. analysing the economy as a whole (in *General Theory of Employment, Interest and Money*, 1936). Using the Great Depression as strong evidence (with 3 million unemployed and no unemployment benefit etc.) that market forces would not, on their own, automatically solve longer-term problems such as unemployment or inflation, he insisted that an economy could not be left to sort itself out. Governments should give up traditional laissez-faire economic policies and intervene in the economy.

Keynes went further, suggesting governments should not keep emphasising production/output/supply, to increase the level of economic activity, but instead should 'manage demand', in order to achieve desired economic objectives, e.g. a significant reduction in unemployment. He developed his theories of **demand management** with what became known as:

Had you heard of him before you started the course?

Is it best to leave a car engine well alone, or keep tuning it?

The Keynesian model of the economy

Aggregate (or total) **demand** = C + I + G + (X – M)

C = Consumer spending – always the largest component of **Aggregate Demand (AD)**, and therefore policy measures will be likely to have significant effects.

I = Investment expenditure by businesses – 'The key to future growth of the economy', so also important, but can be volatile/unpredictable because businesses have their own set of reasons for decisions, e.g. on a new project.

G = Government expenditure – using taxes, and (particularly) borrowing, this is under direct control of a government, e.g. extra millions spent on public sector projects to help boost/reflate the economy [see below].

X = Exports – expenditure by foreigners on domestic products, bringing foreign currency into the UK. They can be encouraged, e.g. by trade fairs, the Queen's Award for Exports, and DTI advice to exporters.

'E' is reserved for Expenditure.

M = Imports – expenditure by British consumers on foreign products, so a 'withdrawal/leakage' from the UK's circular flow [see p. 117, How an economy works], but included because 'X-M' is the international trade sector.

'M' is often used for Money (so Imports go to 'Z'!).

Reflation – policies for when **Aggregate Demand (AD)** has been below the **Aggregate Supply (AS)** potential of the economy (with all its resources fully employed).

Policy instruments include:.

- reducing interest rates (to encourage C and I)   [part of Monetary Policy]
- reducing income tax (to encourage C)   [part of Fiscal Policy]
- increased government spending   [part of Fiscal Policy]
- an export drive (to boost eXports abroad)
- protectionism, e.g. a tariff or quota (to discourage iMports)...if allowed!

Multiplier effects mean that every £1 million injected into an economy increases spending by approximately £5 million.

Deflation – policies for when AD is too high to be matched by the AS potential of the economy, so prices have risen and consumers have bought more imports.

Policy instruments include:

- increasing interest rates (to discourage C and I)   [part of Monetary Policy]
- raising income tax (to encourage C)   [part of Fiscal Policy]

- government spending cutbacks   [part of Fiscal Policy]
- no special encouragement to boost eXports
- no need for protectionist measures (as there will be less spending anyway).

NB There are complications, e.g. raising interest rates may reduce the level of AD, which will in turn usually reduce the inflation rate and the level of imports, but that measure also discourages the important investment by businesses, which is crucial for the future performance of businesses in the economy.

Keynesian policies were adopted by post-war governments in almost every developed economy. Regular policy changes/fine tuning of the UK economy (using deflation then reflation) became known as 'Stop-Go Policy'. Between 1945 and 1970, there was economic growth accompanied by relatively low unemployment and low inflation.

But by the early 1970s there were problems. Economic growth had slowed, even to 'negative growth' (– 0.4%) in 1974, when unemployment rose above 500,000 – considered high. The rate of **inflation** had also gone up, rising to 3.3% in 1964, 7.1% by 1972, a record 16.1% by 1974, and peaking at 26.9% in August 1975!

> *Economic theory had been suggesting that unemployment and inflation would not tend to rise significantly at the same time – a new term was used by economists: 'stagflation' (– a combination of stagnation or lack of growth, and inflation).*

Bacon and Eltis (two economists) published *Britain's Economic Problem: too few producers* (1976), and emphasised Britain's declining competitiveness in manufactures. They concluded that many new service industries did not have exportable products, to bring foreign currency into Britain, to pay for the increasing imports.

By 1976 problems were building further. The pound fell to $2 for the first time ever thus making imported raw materials more expensive. The government was still trying to restrain wage inflation, to control overall inflation, but the trade unions would not accept further such direct 'deflationary' policies (even from a Labour government). In 1978 there followed the 'Winter of Discontent', involving several industrial disputes in key industries, and there were increasing demands for alternative less painful policies that would still solve the economic problems of, particularly, inflation and unemployment.

Supply-side policies

The Conservatives won the 1979 election (and Mrs Thatcher became Britain's first female PM) with a promise of new policies which, like the 'Classical' theories refuted by Keynes, emphasised the **supply-side** of the economy.

Conservative governments, 1979–97, continually emphasised the priority of tackling **inflation**, because of the uncertainty that it caused, e.g. for businesses attempting to forecast costs, cashflow, exchange rates, revenue and profits.

> *'Inflation is the parent of unemployment.'*
>
> Margaret Thatcher (1980).

- Inflation is a general and sustained increase in prices. How is it measured? [see Topic 8 Data and information technology, p. 92 Index numbers].

Mrs Thatcher and Chancellor Geoffrey Howe were persuaded by advisors that the *main* cause of the current inflation problem was UK money supply growing at a faster rate than output in the economy, and increased the emphasis on Monetary Policy as

Understand that...?

International competitiveness is crucial, but becoming more difficult in most markets e.g...?

Uncertainty, e.g. for businesses calculating costs and prices, is the main damaging effect of inflation.

recommended by **Milton Friedman** (Nobel prize-winning economist from Chicago University). They were labelled 'Monetarists'.

Monetary growth limits/targets were set, and the adjustment of **interest rates** became the main policy weapon. By the late 1980s, Chancellor Nigel Lawson was targeting the pound (rather than domestic money supply), and trying to keep it in line with the currency of Europe's strongest economy – Germany (ready for closer economic links in Europe). Interest rates would still be used as the main anti-inflation weapon. The inflation rate was brought to relatively low levels by the early 1990s.

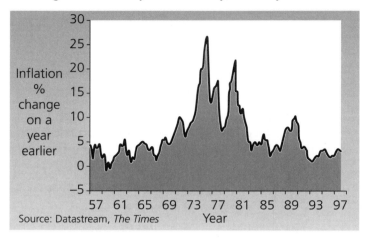

Source: Datastream, *The Times*

'Inflation is like ice-cream. You have to keep licking it.'

John Major (1990).

The Conservatives also insisted that these **supply-side** policies were needed for UK industry to regain competitiveness against other industrialised economies, and protect market shares from low-cost production in several developing countries (e.g. S. Korea, Taiwan and China – the largest economy in the World by 2020). They claimed that the resulting liberalisation of market forces would in the longer-term benefit Britain's leaner and fitter businesses.

'You cannot buck the market!'

Margaret Thatcher (1980).

- **Tax incentives** – e.g. on earned income to encourage people at work (with the rate of income tax being brought down in stages), on profits of smaller (embryo) businesses (with lower Corporation Tax), on employee share schemes, and on allowances for new business investment projects.

- **Reducing benefits** – to encourage people to seek work, and avoid the unemployment trap (i.e. gaining as much income by *not* working).

- **Legislation** – (in 1980, '82, '88, '89, '90 and '93) to free up the labour market and reduce industrial action by trade unions, e.g. abolishing secondary picketing, and holding secret ballots before an official strike, otherwise the union is liable for financial damages from the strike. Critics accused the government of 'union-bashing'.

- **Deregulation and privatisation** – e.g. Post Office Telephones was separated from the Royal Mail and renamed British Telecom, ready for privatisation in 1986. Under supervision from a watchdog, the Office of Telecommunications (OFTEL), it lost its monopoly right to sell telephones and phone calls and was forced to allow competitors to use its lines.

'Rolling back the frontiers of the State.'

Conservative Government (1980).

Can you understand both points of view?

'Selling off Britain's industrial heritage.'

Labour Opposition (1980).

Other privatised public corporations included Cable and Wireless (1981), British Gas (1986), British Airways (1987), Water (1989), Electricity (1990), British Rail (1995), and British Nuclear Fuel (1996).

In September 1998, as allowed by the deregulation of the electricity industry, British Gas plc diversified into selling electricity.

- **Encouraging competition** – referrals to the MMC for reports, e.g. on prices of petrol, coffee and computer games, and several mergers where increased monopoly power might harm the public interest [see Topic 7 Operations management, p. 80 Limitations to growth].

- **Reducing government spending** – to reduce 'crowding out' (of the private sector by the public sector), and reduce government borrowing year-on-year – called Public Sector Borrowing Requirement (PSBR).

- **Increasing emphasis on education and training** – new vocational courses (e.g. NVQs and GNVQs), training programmes (e.g. 'Modern Apprenticeships' for school-leavers, 'Training for Work' for the longer-term unemployed, services provided by the local Training and Enterprise Councils, and the 'Investors in People' award for organisations), plus tax relief on retraining of employees for redeployment.

- **Abolishing wage councils and minimum wages** – to free up wage negotiations and encourage employers to take on more workers (albeit at possibly low pay).

'There can be no doubt that the transformation of Britain's economic performance during the 1980s, a transformation acknowledged by the rest of the world, is above all due to the supply-side reforms we have introduced to allow markets of all kinds to work better.'

Chancellor Nigel Lawson (1988).

In 1990 Mrs Thatcher was replaced as leader of the Conservatives, and PM, by John Major, but claimed that her stated objective of 'leaner and fitter' UK businesses had been achieved.

Critics claimed the cure was killing the patient, in terms of worsening **recessions**.

Deep recessions, e.g. 1979–81 and 1990–93, caused record numbers of **business failures** and high unemployment (up to 3 million in 1985, and still 2 million in the early 1990s). The critics acknowledged the increased productivity in several important industries (e.g. coal and steel), but accused the government of using unemployment as a weapon against wage inflation – workers were more concerned with keeping employment than pushing for higher wages.

'The Organisation for Economic Co-operation and Development is set to downgrade its forecast for economic growth in Britain this year to around 2%. The OECD expressed concern about the UK's relative failure to deal with long-term unemployment and potential social divisions created by a widening disparity of incomes.'

The Times (22/5/96).

The level of unemployment fell steadily after peaking in 1993, but when Labour won the 1998 election they confirmed a commitment to further significant reductions, initially using a special tax on the high profits of several privatised ex-public corporations. In April 1998, when they announced the objective of 'full employment for a new century', there was much discussion on a definition of 'full employment'. Resultant policies will affect businesses.

> *'Top of the list of what the business agenda needs for the next five years must be the need to preserve and reinforce a stable economic environment. Large and small companies agree that stability is critical to all their business planning, investment and financing.'*
>
> Lord Alexander, Chairman of National Westminster Bank, *The Times* (5/9/95).

Keep up-to-date with how businesses are affected, by checking through newspapers (every Sunday if not every day!

The Labour government agreed with its predecessor that keeping a low rate of inflation (maximum 4%) was a priority, to reduce the risks of uncertainty in the economy. A year after they came to power there seemed to be two issues particularly affecting businesses – **interest rates** and **exchange rates**.

Interest rates

- Used as the main weapon against inflation since 1980 (and 'Monetarism').

- The level must keep spending (particularly consumers'), and inflation, under control, but help to avoid problems of a recession (e.g. spending too low).

- Interest rate changes used to be announced by the Chancellor, and banks would then immediately adjust their 'base rates', so different types of lending will then be '?% above base'.

- Chancellor Gordon Brown, soon after the 1997 Labour election victory, made the Bank of England (politically independent) responsible for setting rates.

- Business costs will be affected, because the interest rate is the price of borrowing. Investment projects will thus become cheaper or more expensive.

- Business revenue will be affected when consumer credit, and spending, are encouraged or discouraged by a change in the price of borrowing.

> *'Industry yesterday accused the Bank of England of putting manufacturing in jeopardy after a decision to hold interest rates at 7.25% and a failure to indicate whether they might yet rise. Ken Jackson, General Secretary of the AEEU electrical workers union, said the [Bank's] Monetary Policy Committee's decision to hold rates would "push manufacturing to the brink of recession".'*
>
> *The Times* (22/5/96).

Exchange rates

- The price of one currency in terms of another, e.g. £1 = DM3.0430 (in April 1998).

- Also expressed as an index [see Topic 8 Data and information technology] which includes all the main trade currencies, e.g. the sterling trade-weighted index = 107.3 (in April 1998).

- Determined by relative demand abroad for UK exports compared to domestic demand for imports, and speculation on economic trends, e.g. interest rates.

- Interest rate changes can make UK/sterling investments more, or less, attractive, and affect demand for pounds.

- A volatile exchange rate, i.e. one that is liable to change and is difficult to forecast, causes particular problems, e.g. for businesses trying to predict TR and TC.

- Business costs will be significantly raised, or lowered, by a change in the exchange rate, if a particular business has to import essential raw materials or components e.g. bauxite for aluminium production.

- Business revenue (i.e. number of products sold × the price) will be affected because a change in the exchange rate will alter, favourably or unfavourably, the amount received for each product [see p. 114 The market: Price elasticity of demand] e.g. British Steel exported half its production in 1997, mainly in the EU market where steel is usually sold in German marks – every ten pfennigs the pound rose compared to the mark meant the company would get £100 million less sales revenue. During 1997 the pound gained 60 pfennigs against the mark!

> 'British Steel, which last year began a huge job-cutting programme to cope with the strong pound, called for [interest] rates to be cut. A spokesman said, "We want to see them come down. The pound at this level is making British industry uncompetitive. The value of sterling needs to fall by at least 10%. Analysts expect British Steel profits to nearly halve this year."'
>
> The Times (10/4/98).

The Single Currency

It was agreed by the EU countries that those members who could meet the stated strict economic criteria would be allowed to be part of the Economic and Monetary Union (EMU), based on a single currency – the 'euro', from 1st January 1999. The UK, Denmark and Sweden decided not to join, initially.

Evaluation.

Advantages of joining – for UK businesses (e.g. foreign multinationals which located production facilities in the UK, perhaps to get inside the Single Market):

- Reduced costs of exchanging currencies in the foreign exchange ('forex') market.

- Reduced risks of currency volatility affecting TR and TC [see above].

- 'Price transparency' makes customers aware of competitive prices.

- Many large businesses have already stated they would prefer to deal with suppliers who will accept 'euros'.

- The up-to-date image of a business keeping pace with change.

Disadvantages of joining – for UK businesses:

What is your view? For A level exam questions remember you need to understand both sides/views in order to evaluate properly and get those high marks.

- Some businesses see longer-term risks to the UK government losing many of its economic policy decisions (e.g. on interest rates, which affect the currency!).

- Costly changes to business processes, especially IT systems, and also tills and vending machines.

- 'Price transparency' makes customers aware of uncompetitive prices, previously disguised by exchange rates (a disadvantage?!).

- Many large businesses have already stated they would prefer to deal with suppliers who will accept 'euros'.

This page is for your own notes.

Index